sparkle & GRIT

Live a Technicolor Life By Finally Finding Balance,
Escaping Monotony, and Beating Burnout

Wendy S. Meadows

sparkle & GRIT

Live a Technicolor Life By Finally Finding Balance, Escaping Monotony, and Beating Burnout

Wendy S. Meadows

Edited by Cory Hott and Yna Davis

Copyright © 2023— REFLEK Publishing

All Rights Reserved.

For more information: wendy@wendysmeadows.com

ISBN Paperback: 978-1-7378283-9-6
ISBN Ebook: 978-1-962280-90-7

Dedication

To my husband, Kirk. Thank you for believing in me on the days I lose sight of everything in front of me and get lost in the hard. I appreciate you more than you know for giving me time, space, and the ability to pursue my dreams. For being an equal partner in every stage of life. For being the missing puzzle piece that makes the rest of life make sense and for making my deepest and truest childhood dreams an everyday reality. I don't tell you this enough, but you are my everything. And even though you don't believe it, you are the epitome of GRIT. I love you.

Table of Contents

sparkle & GRIT Resources

Hey there!

Guess what? Before we even get started, I have some presents for you! (How cool is that?) In the chapters ahead, you will notice that I give you some **GRIT-work** exercises. To best set you up to squeeze as much sparkle & GRIT juju juice as you can out of this book, I have created a *free* beautiful and inspirational workbook just for you! This **GRIT-workbook** is the sparkly companion to this book to give you one organized place to delve into the **GRIT-work** as we go along.

In addition to the workbook, I have included other helpful resources, a reading list, and a playlist (and even more goodies and insights to help you along your sparkle & GRIT journey!).

To make it as easy as possible for you to access everything, I have created a QR code so you can conveniently find every resource I refer you to. If the QR code doesn't work (because, you know, technology), you can just type in this address, which will get you to the right place: https://wendysmeadows.com/sparklegritbook

My goal was for you to have a one-stop shop to access all things sparkle & GRIT. If I refer to something in this book that I want you to download, listen to, watch, read, or see, go there and you will find an easy pathway to get it.

And, once you have visited https://wendysmeadows.com/sparklegritbook to download your free workbook, we will be connected!

INTRODUCTION

Dear Reader,

I know we don't know each other (yet), but I am so excited that we have the opportunity to work with one another! I wrote you this book because in my time advising, consulting, and coaching hundreds—if not thousands—of women over the past eighteen years, I have noticed several consistent themes emerging again and again. If I had to condense them all into one sentence, it would be this: We battle burnout constantly (at home, in our jobs, in our personal lives), and usually we have nothing left in the tank for ourselves as individual human beings.

My goal for this book? To give you the tools you need to win the battle against burnout and to *finally* create your version of work-life balance. It has been long enough already, hasn't it?! By following the guidance you will find in this book, you will escape the dreaded monotony and begin to really *live* your technicolor life. You ready?

Are you still not sure if you are burning out (or maybe even already burned to a crisp)? Burnout usually feels like this: You are at your wit's end, about to "pop off" at somebody, and you feel like you are never where you are supposed to be in a given moment. When you are at work, you are worried you haven't been "enough" of a mom that day. When you are at home, you are preoccupied with work. There is never, ever enough time for either.

If I had to give it a visual, I'd say that you might feel like you are on a roller coaster, hanging on to the handrail for dear life with your legs flying in the air behind you and the coaster is going fast, actually increasing its speed, the operator seemingly unaware that you are struggling just to hang on and survive. (Note: While my editor tells me that this would be impossible and defy the laws of physics, I think you see what I am getting at. Anxiety dreams, anyone?)

Instead of finding time to appreciate the life you worked really hard for, to recognize all the schooling, tests, projects, late nights, weekends studying, and working for little pay in the beginning that you went through to get to *this point*, you might be asking, "I worked so hard for *this*? It doesn't feel like I thought it would."

Does any of this resonate? If so, first, welcome to the club! This feeling of burnout is universal, and it has come up in virtually every meeting I have had with every client throughout the years. Yet, while it is a universal feeling, we no longer need to limit our lives by succumbing to burnout. We can win the battle. There is a way out.

I wrote this book to give you my best teachings to beat the burnout in one resource and with one overarching concept: sparkle & GRIT.

Some of what you will read in this book may be things you have already read or heard about a hundred times. I get that. Just as a geometry teacher didn't invent the mathematical science behind geometry, I did not birth personal development. But, before you gloss over a section because you "know it" or "do it" already, I want you to pause. What if something you are doing right now could be 1% better or 1% more efficient? Wouldn't you want to make that happen? Your time is so limited. Think about how that 1% could work for you. Also, even if you already know the life hacks I share in this book, do you truly put them into practice? Even though there are certain things you know you *should* be doing, are you doing them? Finally, when I talk about a concept you know and have heard about several times, take a bet on me that this will be the time it ultimately resonates and sticks. Just like that one teacher you had in high school or college made everything "click," made you say, "Oh! Ah-ha! I get it now!", I am betting this book does the same for you. My aim for this book is to take all the things I have learned, explain how and why they worked for me and my clients, and channel the teachings through one lens (which I call "sparkle & GRIT") so that this is the one book that makes you say, "Oh, this all makes sense now. I can overcome burnout. I don't need to feel guilty anymore. I can define my own version of work-life balance. It is not as hard as I thought. I can do this." And then the magic happens: you freaking *do*.

As I write this for you, I am trying to imagine where you are tuning in from. Perhaps you are reading this while you are in your car, waiting for your kid to finish up soccer practice. Or maybe you have locked yourself in your bedroom, away from the screaming kids and chaos for a hot second of solitude, and, in a moment of frustration, panic, and a bit of excitement, you have decided to crack open this *sparkle & GRIT* book your friend gave you to see what it is all about. Or maybe you are one of my clients already and have embraced taking some "me time" every morning, and you are sipping your coffee on a dark, quiet morning and nestling in with this book before the day begins. Maybe you are on a flight home to California after spending three days in New York for in-person meetings that 100% could have been held via Zoom, and this book caught your eye at the Hudson News while you were picking up some snacks for the plane. Wherever you are coming from, I am just so damn happy you are here. I am hugging you for taking a bet on yourself. I am joining arms with you and ready to walk on the battlefield with you to beat this burnout.

Even though we are just beginning, thank you for taking the time to put yourself first. I know you are so exhausted that you feel it in your bones and the backs of your eyeballs. You can barely see or think straight, and yet you are taking this time for yourself. You know, somewhere deep down in your stomach, that there is more to life, and you are finally ready to find it. Yes!

This book will also address the frustrating monotonous things called life and raising tiny humans. That maddening scenario where every day is different but also the same can be enough to drive you crazy. We wonder how feeling scattered and all over the place can feel repetitive, yet here we are in our own personal version of *Groundhog Day*.

Before we dive in and keep going together, I want to check in and ensure that we "get" each other. I am guessing that when the kids wake you up in the morning and your eyes first see the time on the clock, you think, *Oh, this again?* Then you have the scramble of getting everyone ready and out the door: lunches made, teeth and hair brushed, and dishwasher flipped, all while trying to cobble together a sort of healthy (but also who cares?) breakfast for the kiddos, which you snack on too—because who has the time to prepare one of those Instagram-worthy drooly avocado toasts or smoothies? Meanwhile, you are checking your phone to ensure work didn't blow up overnight and reminding yourself what will be on tap for the day when you walk into your office or fire up your computer. While you are trying to figure that out, you discover that the kids did not fill up their water bottles, their shoes and socks are still upstairs, the bus is coming in five minutes, and all of a sudden, Jolie is fighting with Brandon, the house erupts in screams, and your dog is scratching at the door to be let out. And. You. *Erupt.* You start yelling like a crazy lady that you are "only one person!" and you lose your ever-loving shit on anyone who will listen—cue tears, apologies, hugs, and some more running and rushing.

Magically, somehow, in five minutes' time, the kids make it onto the bus with semi-full water bottles and mismatched socks, but they are wiping away some tears, the dog has been out and in, and you have apologized ten times for losing your temper. You feel pangs of intense guilt because you promised yourself you would parent differently. Now you are even more tired than you were an hour ago. You console yourself by dumping your coffee that has now grown cold on the counter into your travel mug because hey, it's coffee.

Work goes by in a blur. Before you know it, your workday is over. All of the projects you hoped to get done have yet to be started. Your unread email count seems to have doubled throughout the day, even though you felt like an inbox ninja all day, putting out fires left and right. Yet, despite the fact you are behind at work, you are caught up with socials and somehow know what your friends had for breakfast, and you are slightly envious that Liza had the most charming Easter table setting and her children were somehow dressed beautifully for church (with their hair brushed and braided!), and you can't believe how Jennifer is out there showing off her muscles every morning—you have *no clue* how she makes time to work out every damn day and secretly wonder if she is on some sort of drug to give her all of that energy—oh, and Sahmra won her trial today, killing it as always, not only rocking the courtroom but also rocking some freaking amazing outfits (and she is a new mom, what?!). Yet you don't know exactly when your work deadlines are or how far behind you are on specific projects, and there is just so much work piling on top of you that you don't see the path out. But now it is time to fly out the door because you need to be home to get the kids off the bus. Ever since the quarantine, your boss has been allowing you more flexibility and more time at home, and even though you are so grateful not to pay for aftercare anymore, all of it just feels like "*more*" rather than less.

When the kiddos get off the bus, Brandon is there to give you a hug, and it seems like everything from the morning has been erased from his mind, but Jolie is giving you the stink eye. You apologize—again. Even though it is only 4 in the afternoon, you are figuring out a first dinner for the kids because they are starved, but just as you get some leftovers warmed up and on the table, the kids tell you they aren't hungry because they have already raided the pantry and are full on Pirate's Booty, chips, applesauce packets, and the hidden-away Halloween candy. When you go back to the table to pack up the leftovers for later, you discover that the dog already had a free-for-all—the same damn dog who is allergic to everything, whose food costs a hundred bucks for a half bag. Nice, dog, nice. That is going to be fun to clean up in an hour. *Sigh.*

Then, it is off to . . .

Drive drive drive.

Practice practice practice.

Dance. Games. Scouts.

Home. Finally.

Time for a second dinner.

Oh, and even though your partner is present and all four of you sit down at the table, there is no time to have a conversation with him because the kiddos take up so much space. Then, it is finally bedtime. Hallelujah!

You reward yourself with a heavy pour of red wine, some popcorn, and the latest Netflix show, and you sit down on the couch and scroll through work emails. At some point in the middle of the night, you wake up, brush off the crumbs, turn off the TV, make your way to your room, and crawl under the covers.

And you do it again (and again). The cycle feels never-ending. You feel like you must be doing life wrong.

Am I getting this right so far? Or at least some version of it? Maybe your one kid feels like three different children sometimes. Maybe you have five kids, not two. Maybe you have cats that play tricks on you every day. Perhaps you are a single mom sharing custody, and I have just described your life on your custodial days and, and as much as the zaniness is maddening, you also miss it on the days when the kids wake up with their other parent.

I want you to know you are not alone, and you are certainly *not* a failure. You are just tired. Being a mom is exhausting, and not in the way we thought it would be. We thought parents were tired because of newborns' sleepless nights; we didn't expect all of this other never-ending uncontrollable "stuff". Being a working parent feels next to impossible at times. Especially when no one seems to understand that you cannot be in two places at once—if you are staying late at work to make a client happy, then you are letting down your kid, and if you are missing a conference call so you can come home to make sure you are tucking your kid in at night, you are letting down a client. It is hard enough to be fully present for both your kids and your job, and you still need to make food, clean, be on top of the playroom organization, return (okay, and find) all of the overdue library books, fill out fifty medical forms for camp even though you just did all of this last year, book orthodontist appointments, take the dog to the vet, check in on your mother, decorate your home, and make time for self-care.

No wonder you are tired.

I acknowledge that you are tired.

I promise that you are not alone.

Before we go further, we need to breathe. (Don't punch me—I used to hate it when people would tell me, "Wendy, just breathe. *Breaaaaathe*, Wendy."—but really, let's do this.) And I am doing it right here with you. As I am writing this paragraph, I am imagining women all across the globe taking a collective breath, just in this way.

Start by closing your eyes. (Well, read the whole prompt, and then go for it.) Let your shoulders relax. Take them out of your ears. Put your right hand on your heart and your left hand on your belly. I want you to breathe in for three slow seconds, hold for three slow seconds, and then breathe out for six slow seconds. (If six is too long, try for five.) Do that three times. Then read the prompt below.

You are here. You are not alone. We are going to do the work together, right here in this book. Start to see the possibility that life doesn't have to be this way. Start to let go of the "this has to be hard." Begin to embrace that you can have "more" and you are deserving of it. You can show up as the mama you want to be. You can get your work done. It is 100% possible to be 100% present at work and 100% present at home—and to rediscover the you that you really miss, that you know is still in there.

It all starts when you welcome some sparkle & GRIT into your life.

You ready?!

Let's do this.

Love,
Wendy—your coach in all things sparkle & GRIT

I start each chapter with a song suggestion. I encourage you to sit back, close your eyes, and listen to each tune before you begin reading. Or, google the lyrics and read along so you can really hear the message of the song. Either way, let the music help drop you into the feeling of each chapter. To best access the music I suggest, visit the sparkle & GRIT resources; I have already created a playlist for you!

https://wendysmeadows.com/sparklegritbook

CHAPTER 1
Rinse & Repeat

"Something More," Sugarland

What is sparkle & GRIT? Why am I writing this book for you?

sparkle & GRIT is a mindset, a tool, and a concept. It is a state of being. It is a mantra. By the end of this book, my dear reader, you will have defined what sparkle & GRIT means to you.

With the sparkle & GRIT mindset, you can accomplish anything. As you will learn, sparkle motivates and GRIT puts you into action. Using sparkle & GRIT as a tool, you will complete exercises that will help you grow, recognize, and harness the sparkle & GRIT you already have inside of you. Understanding the sparkle & GRIT concept allows you to go through life with an awareness you did not have before, one that inspires and fuels you and that ensures you keep taking action.

Why does it matter?

Because I can clearly remember my own version of *Groundhog Day* and what it felt like to live a life without sparkle & GRIT. I have a mini freakout when I ask myself, "What if nothing had changed? What if I hadn't pulled out of that? What if I never found the sparkle? What if I never learned what true GRIT was? What if I never re-found my GRIT? What if I never put them both together? Where would I be?"

I clearly recall my life before sparkle & GRIT entered the picture. Looking at the road I was heading down, I knew I was on a path to becoming uncomfortable in my skin, in a loveless marriage or divorced, a yelling mommy all of the time, always behind, never feeling like I was living my purpose, and stuck in a job that didn't feel right in my heart.

Not only did the world around me feel gray, but I started acting pretty gloomy myself. I was showing up as tired, bored, whiny, complaining—to my friends, my husband, and goodness knows who else. To anyone who would listen, really, probably even the checkout lady at the grocery store. It got to the point where I started to not like who I was, and I kept asking myself, "Is this really *it*? Is this my life?"

Instead of me telling you all of this, let me show you. Rewind back to 2015. My kids are three and one, and my husband and I have finally gotten them to go to bed and actually fall asleep. It's about 8:30 at night. My husband goes downstairs to watch television in the living room. I follow him, but I go straight to the kitchen, gather my supplies, and head to my room. I do not stop at Go to collect the $200 and actually have a conversation with my husband; I do not kiss him goodnight. Instead, I give him the cold shoulder and escape to my room.

Now zoom in on me, lying under my covers, snuggling down on my nice, comfy Tempur-Pedic mattress with an awesome duvet tucked around me. Yet the bed is headboard-less, and I am surrounded by mismatched sheets and pillowcases with awful dingy yellow walls to match, accompanied by graying white carpet with a massive stain from where I spilled some chicken curry when I decided to have dinner in bed one night. *The Good Wife* is streaming on Netflix. I have a whole tub of Trader Joe's crispy chocolate chip cookies next to me on the nightstand, a bowl of goldfish, and a decent-sized glass of cab franc. Maybe there is a pint glass of water, but I doubt it. I have a cadence to my ritual, and my hands know where to go and how to get to my mouth as my eyes fixate on the TV. I eat a cookie for something sweet, go to the goldfish for that zing of saltiness, and wash them both down with some wine.

Once my glass of wine or bowl of goldfish gets low, I sneak downstairs to the kitchen for a refill (yes, "sneak"). Remember, my husband is in the adjoining living room, also watching TV, and I don't want him to notice I am there. It is not so much about whatever judgment he may have about me pouring another glass of wine. It is more about the fact that I don't want him to realize that I am in the same room, because God forbid he actually tries to talk to me. This is *my* time. I absolutely cannot be bothered. Besides, I am actually learning how to be a better lawyer by picking up new skills watching *The Good Wife*. Also, I had a hard day, so I am totally justified. I deserve this special time of making myself feel good and zoning out, so I don't have to have another thought in my head.

I don't want to wonder what it would be like if I just went to bed early so I could wake up earlier and actually start some sort of workout routine. I don't want to face the fact that I don't love my work life. I don't want to think about how my hubs and I could get back to a better place. I am just so tired. I am too tired to care and snap out of it. I figure staying stuck is the path of least resistance.

But I would be lying if I didn't admit that there is a little burning nudge, somewhere in my gut, that is asking, "Wendy, can't things be different? This isn't you. You know this isn't you. Wake up already. When are you going to wake up!?"

I feel just as awful when I get up in the morning. I sleep for as long as I can every day, not waking until my baby girl cries out for me or my toddler wanders into the room, saying, "Mommy! Cuddle!" Still then, I try to coax them to crawl under the covers with me so we can all get just a teeny bit more shut-eye time. I am tired and fuzzy. I have no energy. The more sleep, the better. I finally make myself start each day around 7:30. Shower, get the kids dressed, throw my sopping wet hair up in a banana clip (remember, this is 2015, back before their 2022 comeback), and get us all downstairs to get the kids' breakfast going.

(Note: I do not feel like a failure at all things. Kid food is one of the things I excel at. My own baby food super-blends? You got it. Eggs, however they want them? Sure! Perfectly balanced meals with cut-up fruit, veggies, oatmeal, and other random concoctions to give the kids the best day possible? I rock those. I take an immense amount of pride when it comes to my kids' food. I say this because I bet you have that one thing too, that one thing that you are insanely proud of.)

Once the kiddos are dressed, fed, and sort of ready-ish, my in-laws arrive to take over, and I can finally go upstairs and get ready for work. I try on outfit after outfit. My body is still changing, as I just finished breastfeeding. My pants are too snug. My shirts don't cover my hips right. My butt feels big and makes my pants shorter in a weird way. My bras are dingy, and the underwire is weird and cut in the wrong place, and I can never get the right cup size because my boobs just went from a DD to a B and then to an A+/B-. It all feels awful, and I mourn the comfort of my elastic-y maternity pants and nursing tanks. (Sidenote: Writing this in 2023, thank *God* for the different pants we have now, just eight years later! Hello, Betabrand! Hello, wearing yoga pants everywhere! Hello, stretchy suit pants! Thank you, thank you!!) Once I finally feel like I look "good enough," off to work I go.

Work is a whole other story. The good news about work? A day in the life of a family law lawyer goes by in a flash! Before I know it, each day is over and it is time to go home and get back to the chaos of dinner, bedtime, and my *Good Wife* friends. In 2015, my workdays are full of calls, emails, meetings, research, court, and hanging out with my family law comrades so that we can bounce ideas off of one another and see how to best help our clients and cases. But, in my heart, there is a niggling feeling that my work environment isn't a place I want to be, nor one where I can stay for the long (long) haul.

Why my job wasn't working? I don't want to belabor this point, but here is what I can tell you: things at my old firm weren't great. As much as my law firm felt like "home" for a really *really* long time, somewhere along the line, things broke. Personalities that used to match clashed. Expectations were unmet in all sorts of ways. At the time I felt like a victim—in some ways I still do—but with hindsight I can also see how I contributed to an environment that no longer worked and bordered on toxic. I knew I was about to reach a breaking point every time I got into the elevator, hit the button for the eighth floor, and felt my heart rate start to pick up speed. I would have to take a big shaky breath every morning as I put my hand on the doorknob to turn it and open the door to our suite. Sometimes it took me a good ten seconds to actually push the door open. In my last year at the firm, I would make a beeline for my office and jump into work emails as quickly as I could so I could avoid "getting into trouble" for goodness knows what. Occasionally I even pretended to be on the phone just to avoid unwanted conversations about nothing. I put my head down, worked really hard, got my stuff done, giggled with the staff I felt comfortable with, plopped down in offices where I truly felt welcome, and then skedaddled out of there to get the kids from the in-laws or from preschool.

This collegiate breakdown, coupled with the question of how long I could be a family law attorney in general, had me very much in my head, questioning my longevity at my firm. You see, I had always had a tug that I wanted to try something else outside of family law. I just had no idea what that "something else" was.

. . . Actually, that right there, that sentence I just wrote, is a lie. I 100% knew what I wanted to do. The day I discovered that being a life coach was a thing, the thought that I could become one immediately lit a fire somewhere deep in my soul. I just had no idea what path to take to get there or how it would all work out. It seemed so impossible and unrealistic. I had zero clue how to break this rinse-and-repeat cycle. I felt so stuck and like any inspiration to try anything else was impossible.

Interesting: even though I've described that whole scenario, I haven't told you what my job actually entailed. Huh, right?

The truth is, I loved my clients (well, maybe just 97.5% of them). I loved hearing their stories. I loved having a concrete way to help them get divorced, gain time back with their kids, or get paid the proper support. More than anything, I loved guiding them through the legal process and being the person to shepherd them through what was likely the worst time of their lives. I absolutely love humans, and learning about human experience after human experience fascinated me. My favorite part of my day was getting to really and truly know my clients, asking them questions no one had ever bothered to ask before, and giving them the space and ear they needed. I enjoyed that I could take an awful experience but still make my clients feel good because they felt heard for the first time in years. Not only did they feel "gotten," but usually, I could come up with and advocate for a solution where they could actually see that divorce could be a better option for them and that life would be better on the other side. My suitemates would comment that clients in my office always seemed to be laughing when they left my office. I had a knack for making my clients feel comfortable, seen, and heard. That was the best part of my job.

The parts I hated?

The yelling. I knew something wasn't right whenever I was on the phone with opposing counsel, someone I was usually also *friends* with, and somehow we found ourselves in a screaming match. *Really?* I wish I could tell you this was a rare occurrence in my field. It's not. There is a lot of yelling—amongst counsel and at clients.

The condescension. The way it dripped from opposing counsel's every word, attacking my client, attacking me, trying to twist up every word to make it look like we were idiots in order to suck the energy away from trying to resolve the matter at hand and instead enter some sort of weird showmanship battle, applauded by no one but their own client (who was paying $400 an hour for these verbal altercations). What a freaking waste.

The other parts I hated? Artificial deadlines. Deadlines I stuck to but my opposing counsel did not, yet somehow it didn't seem to matter. No one actually cared. Meaningless discovery, which cost my clients thousands of dollars, to no end. (Yes, some discovery is 110% worth it and exactly what we need to achieve the best result in a case, but when it is clearly being done to churn a bill, that's not cool.) The wastes of money, the draining of 401(k)s and bank accounts and the accumulation of massive credit card debt that could have been avoided. Seeing so much money spent on legal fees while so little of it actually advanced the ball in any way.

All of that would be enough to drive anyone mad.

And sadly, I was in a weird situation where I felt like I was suffocating every time I stepped foot in the office. There was an undercurrent of toxicity that I could not pull away from. Like I said before, I'm 100% aware that that toxicity was also coming from me. Basically, it got to the point where I couldn't tell if I was the victim or the perpetrator. Probably both. My point? I did not like the person I was becoming.

While I had this secret hope that there had to be something better, I was also convinced that I would have to win the lottery to get there. I was waiting for a miracle to change my life so I could get out of this rut. In a word, I was stuck. And tired. So tired. Eyeballs-hurting-in-the-back-of-my-head tired.

Do you get me?

Do you feel this?

Do you feel it so deep in your bones?

The best sparkly news I have for you? I got the eff out. Of all of that. *All. Of. It.* Without winning the freaking lottery.

Looking back on this period, I now see the miracles—let's call them sparkles—that nudged me out of this funk. But look at the word choice there: "nudge." There was no actual ah-ha moment that slapped me out of that mess and brought me to where I am today. There were no lottery winnings. No bolt of lightning. No fairy godmother. And I have come to learn and realize that this is how the universe/God/our higher power works—through suggestions put in our path meant to wake us up.

I created this book to be one of those sparkles for you, a little something in your path to help get you out of your version of "funk." I cannot wait to teach you everything I learned that helped me pull myself out of that nosedive. But first? I want to show you the woman I am damn proud to be as I write this book. How I am no longer itching out of my skin because I am not living the "right" life. I no longer feel like I am living a lie. I want to show you what my version of happiness is and how I make it a point to find a sparkle in each day.

The awesome news is that I am not even in my final chapter—nowhere close! I am still in and on the journey. I don't have every piece figured out yet. I am still learning, which is why this is the very best time for you to learn with me. Because it is fresh. Because I am still having ah-ha moments as I am expanding a new career path and letting go of an old one. Because not one of us ever stops growing. Nobody (and I mean nobody) has it all figured out, no matter how glamorous and perfect they may appear on your social media feed.

Where am I now and where am I going? I have to be honest, I smiled way more when I thought about the "where I am going" piece because once you accept all of this—that growth is a way of life—it really becomes *fun* and something to look forward to. Growth and change inspire me; they help kick me out of bed in the morning.

It was not always this way. I used to detest change. Change can still scare the crap out of me. But I don't think that is why I am smiling. I am smiling because I know we are going to grow *together*. If you use the principles in this book, you are going to see glorious small nuggets of *life* that you didn't know existed. We are going to put sparkle & GRIT into practice at the same time, and that *thrills* me.

Today? The kiddos are eleven and nine. Bedtime still drives us bananas (I never said parenting was easy or perfect!), but we have a halfway decent routine where our family of four spends time together from dinnertime to the time the kiddos go to bed. I lie with each kid for a short while during their reading time. No longer am I wishing so hard that they would just fall asleep. I have the time and space to ask about their days, and I genuinely want to hear what is on their minds. I am no longer so burned out that I fall asleep in their beds. I am present if they are in the mood to talk and confide in me. If they are having a hard time falling asleep and are in freakout mode, well, those things still do happen, and it is still *hard*, but we are learning, and I am turning to my husband rather than to wine so that we can cope and strategize together.

Once the kiddos are in their beds reading and being quiet(ish), my husband and I decide if we are hanging out together, if I am going to bed early, or if we are both ready for bed. If we choose to hang out together, we watch TV, but sometimes we end up cuddled on the couch just talking before we even pick up the remote. Do I need to actively remind myself to be patient and that checking in with my husband is more important than television? Yes. Am I glad every time I do? Yes. Do I turn in instead of turning away? Yes, every darn time.

If I am going to bed early (most nights of the week), hubs comes with me to tuck me in, and we talk until I can no longer form coherent sentences and I drift off to sleep.

If we both go to bed early, we talk until one of us starts to lightly snore, and then it is a race to fall asleep!

See the theme here? While I am not saying we have marathon conversations, and while I admit that we usually fall asleep mid-sentence, I need to point out that we *talk*. Daily. We connect. Daily. We spend time near each other. Daily. And I look forward to it. We went from a marriage that was quickly losing steam to a marriage where we are each other's best supporters, cheerleaders, and friends. We now complain that we never get enough time together.

How are my mornings different now that I am no longer bingeing Netflix and gorging myself with treats from the Trader Joe's snack aisle?

I am the first person out of bed in the morning. I wake up relatively easily and feel ready to go, anywhere from 4:30 to 5:30. I plug into my tried-and-true routine (more on that in chapter 5). I work out pretty much daily. I follow workout calendar after workout calendar, and I am in better shape at forty-three than I was at twenty-three or thirty-three. Before my workout, I carve out time to plan my day, focusing on the things that really matter the most each day, and then I envision the person I want (and need) to be to show up fully to that most important thing. If I am in creation mode, I write. If I am in learning mode, I read. I take a solid one and a half hours that is just for me—most every morning.

My husband and I both help the kids get ready for school and, through a collaborative effort, all eight hands and eight paws on deck, we get the kids out the door on time with lunches, water bottles, homework, and instruments. I still try to make great breakfasts—if they will let me—but lately, the kids would rather make their own. Sometimes, I walk downstairs to see that they have had a brownie and "something healthy too" already. But when they make a special request for me to make breakfast, I make the time. While I still need to energetically remind the kids about their shoes, socks, bathroom, and water bottles more than I would like, the volume is a *lot* lower. Over the years, my doomsday yelling has dulled to annoying mommy reminders. When I walk the kids to the bus, I hug them one hundred times (while they are still letting me), and I wave until the bus is out of sight. I do not make a mad sprint to get to the next thing, but I take my time walking back up to the house.

Nowadays, I work for myself. I don't rush. I don't panic. I either head to my home office or to my brick-and-mortar office ten minutes down the road. I don't have to dress a certain way (leggings for the win, all day every day!). I don't have to "behave" a certain way. I don't have to justify a day off. I don't feel guilty for having a wacky schedule that is nowhere close to a nine-to-five. I don't answer to anyone but my clients, and I get to choose who my clients are.

My law practice has changed drastically. I went out on my own in 2018 as a solo practitioner. By 2021, I decided that I was no longer litigating cases. My only caveat is that I will still represent children (the reason why I went to law school), so while I may have some trial work, it is minimal. Mostly, when I am working as a "lawyer," you will see me working as a mediator, helping couples resolve their disputes together and coming to a resolution without the need for messy, protracted, and expensive litigation. In mediation, we get to be creative and cost-effective, which only makes me love the work more. August 2023, barring any more postponements, I *should* be ending my career as a "trial lawyer," and August 13, 2023, will mark five years as a solo practitioner. You better believe I will be hosting a celebration!

I am free from a life that wasn't mine to live, even though back in 2015, never in a million years would I have thought I would be able to shed the guilt for long enough to be able to leave my firm. It felt really weird and hard to leave a life that I had worked so hard to create and that I knew was *safe*. Despite my complaints and some of the intrapersonal dynamics, I was part of a firm with a great reputation and I was making decent money. I could have stayed, and it would have been "fine." I get how hard it is to change course when things overall are "fine."

And . . .

I am also doing the work I set out to do when I left my firm. One of the reasons I felt so itchy to leave was because I had just known there was something else for me. I wasn't entirely sure what it was, but I knew I would not have the room to grow and find it if I stayed. Nor would it be fair to the firm if I spent all of that time developing a new business while I was a partner with others.

And . . .

Through some twists and turns, I figured it out. I invested in my first life coach in 2020, became a life coach in 2021, and fell in love with a new way to help humans reach a resolution—this time within themselves. Nowadays, I get paid to carry out my life's passion, which is to *breathe life* into women. Women who are working so damn hard to "balance" it all. To find purpose at work, to be more present at home, to remember what "fun" is, and to *breathe.*

My coaching work? I get to work with women from all around the country. One day, I will be able to say I have coached someone from every US state and even internationally. My coaching calls breathe life into women and, in turn, they breathe life into me. We laugh, cry, and strategize. Slowly but surely, I see my clients gain more confidence, become more effective problem-solvers, learn to be more time-efficient at work and to consistently meet their deadlines, show up fully when at home, begin to exercise, and start that other habit they just know will be good for them.

And my coaching work doesn't stop there. I get to write for a living! (Hello, this book!) I am asked by bar associations and law firms all across the nation to come and speak, give workshops, and host seminars. My new three-year plan? Retreats and a sparkle & GRIT summit—I cannot freaking wait!

And . . .

I don't feel itchy anymore.

I know who Wendy is again.

I remember the best parts of her. I have made peace with the parts of Wendy I have never loved. I show up as fully ME and I can freakin' breathe.

All of the things my past-self dreamed about as a little girl? I am now actually living them.

My rinse and repeat is no longer mindless. I no longer mindlessly do the same thing every day and let life lead me along. No. Now instead, every day I have the beauty of deciding who I want to show up as and how I want to do so, and then doing so with intention.

Now, can I tell you that I am perfect? Heck no. Do I fall on my face? Of course I do. Case in point: in this book, I encourage you to give up weekday wine. Guess what? Yesterday was a Monday night, and guess who poured herself a glass of wine? This girl right here. And even though I have decreased the volume, do I still lose it on my kids and have an adult temper tantrum when I just cannot take it anymore? Yes, it happens. But do I also have some pretty crazy insane wins that have changed my life? *Yes.* Just in these last six months, I have traveled to Arizona, Mexico, and California. Why? Because as a little girl, I always knew I would "travel for work." It looks different than I imagined, but the travel part is very real, and it is happening. Do I have control over my schedule and life? Yes! Do I have beautiful conversations with my kids, and do they have more emotional intelligence than most adults I know and the ability to explain their feelings and thoughts in detail? Yes! Why? Because I did the hard work—I had the sparkles of hope and the tenacity of GRIT to keep taking baby steps until I got there.

I don't show up perfectly all the time. But I show up, and I show up to win, and I do it repeatedly. Why? Because I believe in sparkle & GRIT. I believe that consistently putting in the hard work pays off. I believe it pays off in ways that are so hard and deep we may never even know the actual depth we have created in our lives and the lives of others. I share some vulnerable truths about myself because I know you have some too.

You may even think that this "truth" about you means you aren't ready for a sparkle & GRIT life or that somehow you aren't "enough." Guess what? We all have those thoughts.

And . . .

That. Does. Not. Give. You. Permission. To. Stop. Trying.

You ready?

CHAPTER 2
Overview & Itinerary

"Lose Yourself," Eminem

Have you ever been curious about what life coaching feels like? This is your chance to give it a try. In this book, you are going to learn the same cornerstones, principles, methodologies, and mindset that I use with my clients. And what does it all boil down to? sparkle & GRIT. The method. The mindset. The way you look at the world.

To give you a hint of what that means—sparkle is the *why*, the affirmation, the reason, the butterflies in your stomach that get you out of bed. GRIT is taking baby step after baby step. It's the plan; it's the action that will get you there, even when you don't feel like making any moves.

Note—you will hear me talk about baby steps a lot! Both in this book and in general in my coaching process. Hopefully this gives you some reassurance that I am not going to ask you to take such massive action that you are overwhelmed and frozen in place. When we realize that GRIT is really just talking one teeny tiny step after another, we realize that we can break our goals down into bite-sized chunks and that it is not so scary. Remember the adage, "How do you eat an elephant? One bite at a time."? The same is true for GRIT.

You will note that a lot of what I talk about in this book is geared toward professional female moms, likely those with partners. This is not meant to be exclusionary; it is simply the experience from which I can write. Not every section in this book may apply to you. Some may not resonate with you whatsoever. But in every chapter there will be at least one sentence or idea that will stick with you for the rest of your life. For example, even if you aren't a parent, I can guarantee that after you read the section on parenting, you will walk away with a newfound appreciation for your bestie who always seems to be in the thick of parenting dilemmas.

By the end of this book (assuming you do the **GRIT-work!**), you will have mastered the sparkle & GRIT mindset. You will be sparkle & GRIT-ready for not only the small things that life throws your way (missing the kids' school bus) but the big stuff too (your partner leaving you). Will it always be easy? No. Will you forget some of the principles? Of course—you are human. But will you get back onto that horse a little easier? Heck yes. Will you have a place to refer back to so you can refresh your mind on what you need to do? Yes! You will always have this book and the access to resources.

Before we go further, I am going to give you some tough love. You are likely not showing up as your best self. And while I know you are tired, you *do* have more to give to yourself, your family, and this planet. You have some work to do. Before you chuck this book across the room—and hey, if you need to, I am here for it. Throw it. Jump on it (but then pick it back up)—just know that I am *so* tired too. Also know that, as much as I am going to piss you off, I will be your biggest cheerleader. While I will *not* be the one to blow some toxic positivity smoke up your ass, I will be jumping up and down for you, screaming out your name when you take GRITTY step after GRITTY step. I will be in your head, and there will be a time when you are at a crossroads but you won't be able to get "sparkle & GRIT" out of your head, and you will say, "Damn it, Wendy!" but then you will take action. Even better, once you get the hang of it, you will outgrow me as your coach and won't need to think of me at all. You will just take sparkly, GRITTY action to get closer and closer to your technicolor life.

One more thing. While this book is aimed at professional moms and I want you to kill it in your job and as a parent, there is actually something more important than your roles as a worker and a mom: *you*. You as a person. You on a soul-u-lar level. It has to do with *you* and why you are here on this planet.

sparkle & GRIT—The Short Version

Let's start by defining what the terms sparkle and GRIT mean in this book.

sparkle: the ultimate inspiration; the flame that keeps us going; the source of the visions in the best daydreams; the thing that lights us up. sparkle is that gut feeling tugging us in the right direction so we feel truly aligned with the world. sparkle is a thought or idea that provokes longing, as small as *I should really get healthy* to as big as *I am running for office.*

GRIT: the daily perseverance and action we must call on every day, even if we don't feel like it, that allows us to take small—but consistent—steps toward our deepest desires and to become the humans we know we can be. GRIT is the plan and the action. GRIT is what keeps propelling us forward.

We need both. We need the powerful combination of the two working together. While sparkle and[1] GRIT each contain massive energy, when sparkle & GRIT merge into one concept, you become unstoppable.

Ground Rules

It is important for you to read this book from beginning to end without skipping around. I worked with an amazing team of editors and coaches who helped me organize this book (talk about a GRITTY process) so that it would have the biggest impact possible on you.

There is **GRIT-work** at the end of each chapter (and sometimes in the middle). As you might be guessing, **GRIT-work** is your "homework." If you love homework and digging into all things personal development–related, then I know you are already pumped about this and **GRIT-work** will 100% be your jam. If you are thinking, *Oh no, another thing to add on to my chaotic life? Do I really have to do it?* then tough love answer? Yup, you really have to do it. Doing the work and digging deep is what is required to spark real change, and finding a new way to approach life is *why* you are reading this book in the first place, right? Remember, "nothing changes if nothing changes."

Remember how I told you at the beginning of this book that I created a companion workbook (the **GRIT-workbook**)? The beautiful thing about the **GRIT-workbook** is that it has all the prompts and exercises I include in this book laid out for you, so you have an easy and aesthetically pleasing way to get down to business. In addition to the

---

1. Notice the intentional "and" instead of "&." "&" merges the words "sparkle" and "GRIT" together into one concept while "and" looks at the two entities as separate and existing on their own.

prompts, I threw in some other fun visuals, exercises, and illustrations to tie it all together.

If you have not downloaded the **GRIT-workbook** yet, what are you waiting for?! Go to https://wendysmeadows.com/sparklegritbook or scan below before going any further!

In case you are thinking about plowing through the book and "saving the **GRIT-work** assignments for later," which we both know will not happen, you must take a hard stop each time I give you an assignment. Sometimes this will mean cracking open your **GRIT-workbook** and getting down to business (usually when I am asking you to write out your answers to specific questions or prompts). Sometimes it will mean opening up your calendar and scheduling a task or a reminder to get your **GRIT-work** done later that day if it involves a call to a business or a friend. Sometimes it will mean just stopping, thinking, and being aware—in those cases, maybe you are taking time to create a sticky note for your bathroom mirror to give you big overall reminders. Don't overthink this. You will know if you are cheating. Trust that little voice in your head; she will lead you in the right direction.

Set yourself up for success. When is the best time of day for you to read this book and do the corresponding work? I highly suggest making this a part of your morning routine and gifting yourself with twenty to thirty minutes a morning to read and do the work. This is the best way to have an uninterrupted reading session (and it's a great way to start each day!). While doing your **GRIT-work** that requires some sitting, thinking, and mental elbow grease, consider the following tips . . .

- Cozy up with your favorite coffee or tea next to you;
- Sip on a giant bottle of water to stay hydrated;
- Silence your phone;
- Take off your smartwatch;
- Turn off the TV;
- Show up as your true self;
- Don't feed yourself BS;
- Be coachable;
- Be willing to learn;
- Be willing to get uncomfortable;
- Be willing to try new things.

Remember, you picked up this book for a reason. You know you have sparkle & GRIT inside of you, and you are ready for it to come out!

Let's go!

CHAPTER 3
The sparkle & GRIT Mindset

"Courage," P!nk

What is this magical thing called sparkle & GRIT, and why does it matter?

In order to carry out the life we were put on this planet to live, from the small moments in time to the big, grandiose, audacious actions we must take in order to fully show up and be present, we need both sparkle & GRIT.

Remember the definitions I just shared with you in the previous chapter? I'll repeat them here:

sparkle: the ultimate inspiration; the flame that keeps us going; the source of the visions in the best daydreams; the thing that lights us up. sparkle is that gut feeling tugging us in the right direction so we feel truly aligned with the world. sparkle is a thought or idea that provokes longing, as small as *I should really get healthy* to as big as *I am running for office.*

GRIT: the daily perseverance and action we must call on every day, even if we don't feel like it, that allows us to take small but consistent steps toward our deepest desires and to become the humans we know we can be. GRIT is the plan and the action. GRIT is what keeps propelling us forward.

We need both. Without sparkle, GRIT is pointless. Without GRIT, our dreams never become a reality.

The sparkle & GRIT mindset starts with a sparkle of inspiration and usually begins tenuously. sparkle begins in the form of a question or consideration and begins with "what if," "could I," or "maybe if I." For example,

"What if I started that podcast?"

"What if I signed up for piano lessons?"

"Could I leave this job and start my own company?"

"What if I went on that women's retreat that keeps popping up on my Instagram?"

"Could I join that yoga studio down on the corner?"

"Maybe if I speak up at work, I would get to take the lead on that case."

"Maybe if I stopped hanging out with Susie, I would stop feeling so negative all the time."

"Maybe if I left my marriage, my kids and I would start thriving."

The sparkle stirs up longing. She hits a nerve. She flips your stomach. If you are not ready for her, she can start an anxiety spiral. The trick, however, is to allow the sparkle to grow and to see her in her full glory, without judgment or fear. To consider giving her some life. To explore her. To fan the flame until you feel sparkles bubbling up all through you. To allow yourself to get excited with the possibility. To not let fear get in the way.

Yet we need more than sparkle alone. Without action, she is just a fantasy. Just a wish. We can think about her and dream of her, and while that is the perfect beginning, it is not enough.

We need sparkle's partner: GRIT.

GRIT was first conceptualized by Angela Duckworth, PhD. Duckworth explains GRIT as "passion and perseverance for long-term goals."[2] In her book *Grit*, she also explains that the type of people she observed with grit were "resilient and hardworking" and knew "in a very, very deep way what it was they wanted. They not only had determination, they had *direction*."[3] If you are worrying you aren't "GRITTY" enough and are already ready to throw in the towel because nothing you have done has worked before, stop that. This book is going to help you turn on your GRITTY self. You are going to build your GRIT by sitting down and doing your **GRIT-work**. Together, we will build that GRIT muscle so it works long after we are done with our work together.

GRIT is taking baby step after baby step to walk along the path to get to our dream. GRIT is our action plan, our perseverance, our structure, rules, and strategy. GRIT is perseverance. GRIT looks like . . .

- To-do lists
- Action plans
- Spreadsheets
- Showing up when we don't want to
- Doing the homework
- Dogged determination
- Getting the thing done

---

2. "FAQ," Angela Duckworth, accessed July 13, 2023, https://angeladuckworth.com/qa/.

3. Angela Duckworth, *GRIT: The Power of Passion and Perseverance* (New York: Scribner, 2016), 8.

We need both sparkle & GRIT to achieve our life's goals, no matter how big or small they are. sparkle & GRIT can help you yell less at the kids, and it can also help you leave a job you no longer love. sparkle & GRIT together is what wakes you up and gets you moving. With the sparkle & GRIT mindset, everything becomes clearer. You will start to feel more alive, and you will have a plan.

Diving More Into sparkle

sparkle is our "why." sparkle makes our hearts sing. sparkle is the joie behind the de vivre. sparkle is laughter. sparkle is magic. sparkle is that thing you are missing and you aren't quite sure what it is and then it is there and you are like ah-*ha*—that is it!

sparkle can reveal herself as a gift on our path, put there to wake us up. A sign. A question. An idea. A callout. Again, all designed to *wake you up!* To stop you in your tracks. To pull your gut in a way that feels different from everything else. sparkle shows us that our lingering dreams or wishes have some true possibility. You know how you can point to a few defining moments in your life? The way you feel in those moments is usually sparkle talking.

It was a week after Christmas, probably in 2016 or 2017. I was pumped because one of my besties from high school, Elizabeth, and her girlfriend, Stefanie, made the trek to visit me and my family in the boonies. That night, my husband took over bedtime duty, and the three of us opened some wine and sat in the living room sharing work war stories. This was a time when I was feeling particularly itchy, as I had succumbed to the realization that it was time for me to leave my job, but I was absolutely paralyzed on how that would even happen. I remember complaining to Stef, saying, "If only I could win the lottery, then my life would change."

The next moment will be seared into my memory for life. Stef looked me dead in the eye with an inquisitive, impish smile and shot back, "But do you really need to win the lottery to make that happen?"

Something about her words and the way she delivered them sent a jolt to my heart and mind—sort of like an AED machine. In that moment, I began to wake up. And you already know how that story eventually turned out.

Another one of my favorite sparkle moments was back in 2017, right as I was beginning to become aware of the sparkle & GRIT mindset. I had always wanted to do one of those Spartan races where you run around a hilly countryside, stopping only for some insane obstacles and getting crazy muddy. I was a cross-country runner for all of high school and some of college, so the idea of taking a "break" during a race was intriguing. Every time I heard about a friend doing one of those races, I felt a hint of envy. "Could I do that?" "What if?" Sometimes I would sit there and Google, find a race, start to sign up for it, and then chicken out when I got to the checkout page. How was I going to learn how to climb a rope? Use monkey bars? As cool as the races looked, I didn't see how I would be able to get through one. I would sigh, shut off the computer, and walk away. While that would make me feel a little sad, there was usually a kid calling out for me and needing me anyway, so I would just forget about it and go back to the humdrum of everyday life.

One spring day, I was scrolling Facebook, and I saw that my old trainer at the local gym was hosting a small group class over the summer, all dedicated to training for the Spartan.

That post right there? It ignited my spark. All of a sudden, the lurking thoughts of *Could I figure out the obstacles in a Spartan?* turned into something more tangible: *What if I signed up for Erin's class? I could finally have a way to train for a Spartan in the right way! I might actually succeed?!* Without overthinking it, I sent my trainer the $155 (I love an early bird registration), signed up for the most local Spartan Race I could find, and felt butterflies of excitement bursting out of my chest. Writing this, I can still feel them now. Telling you the story is getting me excited all over again. My breath is a little shallower, my stomach is flip-flopping, and I am sitting here and wondering . . . *what if I did it again?*

But back to my story! With Erin, I was able to train hard for that race. My training was GRITTY, messy, and raw. Erin had me running trails in my neighborhood that I had never known existed, trudging up insane power-line hills, doing sandbag carries and bucket runs, and monkey-barring on all the local kids' playgrounds—and she taught me how to climb a damn rope. She didn't blink at my torn-up hands, and she high-fived me when I was sufficiently tired and muddy, a bit scraped up, and oh so sore. Training for that race was GRIT.

Enter race day. Each and every obstacle was about ten times harder than the ones we had trained on. The monkey bars were spaced crazy far apart, the rings came right after a quarter-mile seventy-pound gravel bucket carry up and down crazy hills, and the six-foot wall was indeed six feet with no footholds (cue thirty burpees multiple times over—if you know you know). Then came the rope climb, close to the end of the race. It was higher than any rope climb I had ever done before, but I was ready. I knew how to do this. I knew the right-foot-circle-and-inch-up method. But then . . . I got two-thirds up the rope and realized I was *high* up. Super high. At this point in the race, who knows how many burpees I had done, how many miles I had logged, or how many feet I had crawled? My hands began to loosen, my arms trembled, my legs started to shake. The ground was far away, and I was tired.

I took a breath. I stopped. I thought about sliding back to the bottom and just doing the thirty-burpee penalty. But then I heard Erin, scream, "Don't stop! You got this, Wendy! *Your daughter is watching you.*" I looked down, and sure enough, there was Erin, standing with my husband and my kids. (Yes, now I am crying writing this—talk about how that sparkle can stick with you.) Damn skippy if that didn't push me to the last ten feet of that climb to ring the damn bell. Damn skippy if I didn't wave to my coach and family, fist raised, and then slide (thank God I was wearing gloves) the whole way down. The smile on my face, the tears in my eyes, the swelling in my chest, the *magic* I felt. That right there was the sparkle. That utter feeling of being *alive*, accomplished, victorious. That is sparkle on crack. That is what we are going for. Making those super sparkle memories where we know we are living *life*. Creating moments that are evidence that we are living the life we worked damn hard for. Those are keepers.

See how sparkle showed up strong at the beginning and the end? sparkle moved me into action, GRIT took over with a plan, and then sparkle showed back up *hard-core* when my goal was met. The Spartan wasn't about just finishing the race; it was about the feeling I wanted to experience during the race, the fun, the pride. It was about showing my family that I was more than a mom, about demonstrating for my daughter that women are strong and powerful and can do hard things.

My most recent sparkle moment?

Summer of 2022. Less than a year ago. I was walking outside on a sunny day, getting some me time in the form of vitamin D, step count, and podcasts. As I was scrolling through suggested podcasts, I landed on one simply because it had the word "legal" in it. During the episode, the host talked about a conference she was putting on in Phoenix, Arizona, called "Dream Bigger." *That sounds intriguing*, I thought. Throughout the rest of my walk, sparkle was bubbling, and my gut was telling me that I had to attend this event—period. As soon as I got home, I raced to my computer, googled dates, put them on my calendar, and booked a flight to Phoenix. Mind you, I had no idea who this lady was who was hosting the conference, nor did I know what the conference was about (except for "dreaming bigger"). But that three-day conference changed my life. As I listened to speaker after speaker, it was like the whole event was curated just for me. I sat front and center. I listened with rapt attention. Instead of thinking, *This maybe, sort of, kind of, could be me*, I thought, *This conference was made for me, and I want what they have. They are my future. I can do this too. I WILL do this too. Let's go!* During the same conference, I was introduced to several individuals who have pushed me, expanded me, and helped me grow in insane ways. It is because of them that I was able to write and publish this book.

Keep in mind, I just went to the conference in October of 2022. As I am typing this sentence, it is currently May 3, 2023. *Seven months.* That is how fast sparkle can flow through and catapult you—if you let it.

What Is GRIT?

"GRIT." It's a fun word, isn't it? It evokes a raw, tough power. But what does it really mean? Remember, Duckworth's definition of GRIT is "passion and perseverance for long-term goals." She also tells us that "grit is about having what some researchers call an 'ultimate concern'—a goal you care about so much that it organizes and gives meaning to almost everything you do. And grit is holding steadfast to that goal. Even when you fall down. Even when you screw up. Even when progress toward that goal is halting or slow."[4]

My view of GRIT is a bit different. I think you might like it because you may be saying to yourself, "I have no freaking clue what my long-term goals are. Right now, my goals are keeping my kids alive, keeping my sanity, and keeping decent enough food in the fridge. My hope is that this book helps me with work-life balance, and I am not quite ready to think long term. I am just here for help with the shit show I have going on now."

Good, I got you. Try this on:

GRIT is *how* you approach each and every day, day in and day out, even when it is mundane. GRIT is baby step after baby step, even when the end is not in sight. GRIT is showing up, even when you don't want to. GRIT is that inner tenacity that already got you this far. GRIT is consistently getting back up and moving forward, no matter how many times you get knocked down and backwards. GRIT keeps going.

GRIT looks like not popping off at someone.

GRIT looks like journaling in the morning, even if you have a million things to do.

---

4. Angela Duckworth, "Angela Duckworth on True Grit," interview by Katie Couric, Katie Couric Media, April 29, 2019, https://katiecouric.com/culture/2122-2/.

GRIT looks like thinking about *who* you want to be that day and writing it down.

GRIT looks like turning down a second glass of wine and going to bed instead.

GRIT looks like not looking at social media right when you wake up.

While I am still going to push you in this book to think about and set some longer-term goals, I am fully aware that just simply existing may be front of mind right now. Let's find the small ways to be GRITTY and then go for the bigger things.

It's time to state your commitment to being GRITTY, right here and now. I want you to read the following paragraph out loud. Really, do it. No one is listening. Or go drive your kids nuts and say it in front of them (that's my style).

> *I commit to showing up. I commit to trying new GRITTY things. I will take baby step after baby step. I will commit to a plan. I give myself permission to start slow. I will persist. I will remain steadfast. I am a GRITTY person because I am taking ACTION.*

The Nitty-Gritty of GRIT—The Roles of Willpower, Habits, and a Plan

I have a client who sometimes tells me that she doesn't have enough "willpower," and therefore she must not have what it takes to be GRITTY. Good news: willpower alone is for the birds. When was the last time you beat yourself up because you didn't have enough willpower to say no to Ben & Jerry's at 10 p.m.? Of course you didn't have any willpower that late at night. Did you know that, according to scientists, our self-control is "like a muscle that gets tired from exercise," which gets worn down and "sapped by the many decisions, distractions, and stresses we face" each day?[5]

What does that mean in plain language?

Once we have worked our asses off all day long, already out of bed too early because while the kids slept in until a reasonable hour, the dogs did not . . . once we have dealt with fire after fire at work . . . ran our kid's instrument and forgotten lunch to school . . . flew into the pickup line . . . scrambled together dinner . . . checked email for the zillionth time to make sure we didn't miss a response from an important client . . . and now that the kids are finally sort of asleep in their rooms . . . at this point, even the scientists are saying that we do not possess the *willpower* to say no. There is nothing in the tank, and Jiminy Cricket went to bed long ago.

Saying that you are lacking willpower is *not* an assault on your human character. Of *course* you are lacking willpower. We are on the brink of burnout every damn day. All the energy that would need to activate that willpower muscle is being spent elsewhere, on keeping us and our kids alive.

Yet this newfound realization does *not* let you off the hook.

Ouch, I know.

But before you throw this book across the room again, find hope in what I am saying. There is nothing wrong with you. There is nothing wrong with the level of willpower you have. In fact, I am telling you to throw the concept of willpower out the window!

---

5. Kelly McGonigal, "Five Temptations That Actually Boost Your Willpower," *Psychology Today*, April 12, 2012, https://www.psychologytoday.com/us/blog/the-science-willpower/201204/five-temptations-actually-boost-your-willpower.

Gone are the days of "muscling through it" and saying things like "I just need to try harder." Beating yourself up because you never feel like you have it together is over. That mindset that you are not good enough or that something is wrong with you stops here. It is time to start afresh and to adopt a GRITTY mindset.

But how?

By building habits. Journaling affirmations. Carrying out routines. Looking at the smaller picture. Showing up to the smaller tasks.

Chunking it down.

Repeating it day after day.

In the following chapters, we will develop the routines you need to make sure you are becoming the most GRITTY version of yourself. You will learn to speak to yourself in a loving way and to start each day with an affirmation to ensure you are 100% showing up as the best possible you for the unique day you have ahead. You will show up again and again, stacking on new routines, one baby step at a time, and before you know it, you will have developed several new habits.

What will these habits do? Increase your GRIT.

Growing Your GRIT

I wasn't born with a GRITTY mindset. In fact, I can remember in vivid detail so many of the times I quit on myself—more times than I can count.

1996. I was captain of the cross-country team, and my high school traveled all the way to Washington, DC, to run an invitational at Georgetown Prep. About two miles into the race, I caught an awful side stitch cramp. It slowed me down fast, and my opponents and fellow teammates began to pass me. I quickly lost any lead I had, and as I did, my confidence flew right out of me. Instead of GRITTING it up,

I stopped running. I walked off the course and quit the race. If I recall correctly, I blamed my ankle, but that was a lie. I was too embarrassed that my time would be slow and figured it would be better to have no time at all. I had zero GRIT that day. It felt awful.

Ten years later, my friend Bettina convinced me to sign up for the National Half Marathon. A few miles in, I looked down at my watch and saw that we were running way faster than we had originally aimed to (we had talked about trying to keep a pace just above nine minutes per mile). We were crushing 8:40s! My first thought was that there was no *way* we could keep this up. We were going to hit a wall!

I yelled over to Bettina, "We're going way too fast! We'll never be able to keep this up!" She just flashed me a determined smile and some sort of motivational "atta girl, let's do this" response. While my initial reaction was like, *Heck no! I am just going to let her go ahead and she can run like a madwoman, and I can just drop back. She will understand. It will be okay. I can shift gears to something more reasonable . . .* I didn't. 2006 Wendy was GRITTIER. She had been through more shit. She knew what it was like to feel defeated. She knew what it felt like to overcome. She had been through the ringer time and time again, and she was stronger.

With dogged determination, I kept putting one foot in front of the other, matching Bettina's pace for *miles*. I was able to keep up with her all the way to the 12.5-mile mark, at which point that crazy woman sprinted to the end. I had been running so fast for so long that I legit did not have a 0.6 mile sprint in me.

Once I was outside of Bettina's eyesight, I could have dropped back, finally slowed my pace, and just limped over the finish line, but I didn't. I kept pace until mile thirteen and then sprinted in the last 0.1, breaking all my personal records.

Do you see how my GRIT grew in two ways? First, it propelled me to run faster, even when I had a valid excuse to slow down. Then it propelled me to finish my race with pride and determination, even when Bettina smoked me at the end. GRIT takes time, but if you keep showing up and going after new challenges that push you, it grows.

As you can see, GRIT is a muscle I have built over time. I did not let that one race, or the many times I have fallen on my face after it, define me. Instead, I wake up each day and ask, "How I can do better? Where can I be a GRITTIER person?"

Why Do We Need Both sparkle & GRIT?

As I mentioned above, we need both sparkle & GRIT. Even though each one is super amazing on its own, think about what would happen if you just had sparkle and no GRIT? You would be excited about things! You would have dreams! You would know your innermost desires. Yet, without action to drive them home, would you ever actually get to experience all of those dreams you have dancing around your head? What about if you had a life that was just full of GRIT? Sure, you would take action, work hard (so hard), and keep moving forward, but for what purpose? Would you even know why you were working so hard? Would it even matter? Would you be aligned with your ultimate goal? Would you have an ultimate goal, or would you just show up every day and GRIT it out and move forward, but to destination nowhere?

Do you see how sparkle & GRIT are both necessary to help you both dream the dream and achieve it?

But it is even more than that. When you combine sparkle and GRIT, it creates an exponential synergy. The concept of synergy means the whole is greater than the sum of its parts. Meaning if sparkle = 2 and GRIT = 2, sparkle & GRIT = 10+! When you embrace the concept of sparkle & GRIT, your growth and abilities will become limitless.

sparkle & GRIT: a synergetic concept that combines inspiration and perseverance into limitless potential and growth. Those who employ a sparkle & GRIT mindset and do the **GRIT-work** will find success in breaking free from monotony, beating burnout, and finding balance and will realize that they are well on their way to living a technicolor life.

GRIT-work

Answer these questions.

1) Why are you reading this book?
2) What are you hoping to learn from this book?
3) What are you hoping to change about yourself?
4) What habits are you hoping to pick up?
5) If you can make a change and pick up a new habit, what will that mean for you?
6) What else will that affect?
7) If those things start happening, then what?
8) Who does that affect?
9) Why will that make your/their life better?
10) What will that mean in the big picture?

Read over your notes. Are you seeing a movie play before your eyes? Really picture yourself in the movie you just created. What is the story you see in front of you when you look at the big picture? Are you envisioning life in a new way?

Now close your eyes, take a breath, and really *see* all of that unfold and come to life behind your eyelids. Daydream, and pay attention to what you are doing in that daydream. How are you interacting with your family? What does your work look like? Look around and see all of these little changes happening for you. See it all play out.

Now take a minute and turn inward. Take a seat in your daydream (like a dream in a dream—*Inception*-style). Take a deep breath in. Let it out. (Again, in . . . out . . .) How are you feeling? Is a smile spreading across your lips? Do your shoulders feel a little lighter? Do you have a fluttering feeling in your chest?

Now answer these questions:

1) If you can see yourself in the prompt above, what does she have that you want?
2) How is that different from what you have now?
3) Why do you want it?
4) What will that mean for you, your family, your friends, your work?

Write it all down.

Look back at the answer to that last question. What will all of this *mean* to you if you can make it all happen? Does that bring a tear to your eye? Does it make you want to laugh gleefully—and also want to vomit? If yes, that is your *why*. The *why* is your sparkle.

All of those good feelings of seeing yourself grow along the way, the smiles, the benefits for your family, for your loved ones. The small wins. The big wins. That is the sparkle.

GRIT is nothing without a why. GRIT is nothing without the sparkles along the way.

Why work so damn hard if you have no why guiding you?

And . . .

We need the GRIT to make us work, show up, and get things done. The GRIT gets shit done—the sparkle makes it all worth it.

It Starts and Ends with You

Before you get too nervous and think you don't have sparkle & GRIT in you; before you start worrying you don't have what it takes to live a life of sparkle & GRIT; promise me you will keep going and keep reading. I assure you, you do.

If you are worrying that your why is not "enough" or, on the flip side, that your why is too crazy big and absurd, I promise you, it *is* enough, and it is *not* too big.

And guess what? Right now (yes, *right the heck now*), we get to make a decision to move from bleak to brilliant, to know we are "enough," to claim that we are deserving, to live a life of sparkle & GRIT—or, to use one of my favorite ways to describe the transition, to transform from one hundred shades of gray to technicolor. Because when you begin to see life in technicolor, all of the small and big moments become increasingly more vivid and rich. Beauty is everywhere. Life becomes more wondrous, exciting, and you want to hop out of bed to experience it rather than just power through to the next thing. Do you see the magnificence of a technicolor life?

And let me make sure I say this before we go any further:

You are perfect the way you are. You are perfectly you. *You* are already an amazing human being. There is no one else on earth just like you. You are already 1 in 784,638,462,784,627,462,873. You are meant to be here. *You* are just right. You as a human freaking being matter.

And we can still do some work together.

Still don't believe me?

Still nervous about whether you have "enough" in you to do the work this book requires?

Think about your favorite person in the world. Why do you love them? Are you ready to see them reach their full potential? Do you see them holding back and want them to shoot for the moon? Even knowing all of their faults, do you still believe they could be wildly successful if they put their mind to it? Do you *know* they are capable of sparkle & GRIT? Even if they have been less than "perfect" at times? Even when they make mistakes? Even when they hurt your feelings?

Guess what? I can guarantee someone else in this world feels the *same way about you*. You are already enough *and* you are capable of the life you want. You are deserving of all things sparkle & GRIT.

This means you also owe it to yourself—an already insanely wonderful human being—to *level up*.

CHAPTER 4
Break the Groundhog Day Cycle

"9 to 5," Dolly Parton

It is time to break the vicious cycle of rinse and repeat. It is time for us to find *you*.

Now, before you go rolling your eyes and thinking, *I never knew I was lost*, hear me out. This chapter will give you actionable methods to remember your most favorite parts of yourself. *You* as a person, before you were a mom or a badass professional woman.

What Is Your Status Quo?

First up, we need to outline your version of Groundhog Day. In the introduction, I took a guess at what that might look like, and in chapter 1, I shared my 2015 version with you. Now it is time to figure out your Groundhog Day story.

It is time for some **GRIT-work**. Stop what you are doing and grab your **GRIT-workbook**!

For this exercise, write down your day from start to finish. Think about the tasks, chores, events, emotions, highs, lows, exciting things, and frustrations that happen again and again, day in and day out.

Here are some prompts to help you along:

1) What time do you wake up? How do you wake up? Naturally? To a blaring alarm? To the kids jumping on your bed? How do you feel when you wake up? Are you groggy? Energetic? Sweaty? Cold? Who is in bed next to you?

2) What is the first thing you do? Check email? Groan? Hop out of bed to walk the dogs? Soothe a crying baby? Snap at a partner? Cuddle? Go back to sleep?

3) Once you are walking around, where do you go first in your house? On your walk there, what are you thinking about? How are you feeling? Where are you feeling those feelings in your body as you walk around?

4) Do you work out? What sort of workouts do you gravitate toward? Do you think about working out and then choose not to? What do you tell yourself when you are thinking about working out and deciding not to? Do you talk yourself out of it? What is the mantra running through your brain?

5) How long do you have from wake-up until you need to be at work?

6) Is work a commute away, or do you work from home? How do you feel when you get in the car?

7) When you step into your office, are you excited to get into work? How do you feel when you sit at your desk? Nervous to open email? Annoyed that you have coworkers? Super excited to see your fave coworker or work husband?

8) Walk yourself through your workday. What is the annoying thing you do every day that you don't love? What is your most favorite part of your job?

9) When you leave work, where are you going? What do you do first?

Now, I want you to go through and read this **GRIT-work**.

1) What is coming up for you?
2) In your current version of Groundhog Day, do you spend any time on self-care? Do you have any "me time"?
3) I want you to highlight the parts you *love* about your life and do not want to change. I want you to circle the parts you know it is time to change and do some work on.

Awesome! Now we have a baseline.

Sometimes my clients start to feel nervous when we do an exercise like this because they are scared that it is pointless because there is no *way* that the circled parts will *ever* change. They feel that they are stuck and there is no way out. I can pretty much guarantee there is a way, I was there too. I was stuck for years, but I got out. Once you figure out your sparkle and once you apply the GRIT, each day, your ability to get unstuck will be more of a reality than you ever realized.

Going Back in Time

Let's time travel.

When I am working with a client, this is one of my favorite exercises because I see their face light up and I get a peek into the version of "them" who first felt "alive!" as a young adult. Often when I do this exercise, the "favorite" part of self is tied to a time where a person first had a taste of freedom as a young adult.

The **GRIT-work** in this section is dedicated to remembering who we *are*. Usually, it is that person we were before we were a wife and before we had kids.

When I do the following exercise, I usually find myself with a video clip in my mind that takes me back to 1997. In that mind movie, I can see the peppy, bubbly, sparkly me that was coming alive. I was a junior in high school (AHS—yes!) and I remember weaving through the crowded hallway, leaving my Functions and Statistics class and heading to the other side of the school for gym. I guess I wasn't all that sparkly on that particular day because Eddie, one of my running buddies, said something along the lines of, "Wen! What's going on? I'm used to seeing you smiling and bubbly all the time. You okay?"

Why is it this movie that sticks out for me, and why is it important to help me remember who Wendy was as a person? In that moment, I felt seen. It was like Eddie held up a mirror to my best self and the person I wanted to be. Rather than a peer seeing me as ditzy or silly or dorky or awkward (all characteristics I had struggled with ever since my family had moved back to the States from Scotland when I was in third grade) one of my friends who I looked up to and respected saw *me*.

Now, while I am not a fan of relying on outside validation to tell me who I actually am, this moment was different. I felt like the person living inside of me was finally also on the outside. While you will hear me tell you until I am blue in the face that *your* opinion of you matters the most, I cherish this particular memory because it gives me a peek into who I was as far back as 1997. It also tells me that I need to time travel back to 1997 and see what I was doing and then find what was working.

I remember how my days went with some scary accuracy.

My sparkly routine went something like this:

6:03	Awake! Shower and get ready for the day.
6:15	Gel and scrunch curls, just so. Apply silver eyeliner.
6:30	Toast sesame bagel with butter for breakfast.
6:35	Read a book in quiet solitude, with no one yelling at me.
6:45	Pour a glass of mandatory milk with four rationed[6] Famous Amos cookies.
7:05	Best friend picks me up, and we drive to school.
7:15–7:25	Hang out with my boyfriend and our friends in the band room.
7:30–2:00	Class.
2:00–3:00	Student government meetings/Choir rehearsals/ Shenanigans with my cross-country and track teammates.
3:00–5:15	*Hard* cross-country or track practice with coaches I adored.
5:15–6:00	Prolonged ride home with good friends from cross-country and track.
6:00–6:30	Dinner.

---

6. My stepfather had a very utilitarian/frugal/no-food-waste approach to grocery shopping. We only bought exactly what we needed each week. What did that look like? I had to carefully ration my cookies for the week so I would have enough for my breakfast milk (he also made me drink a lot of milk!) and my lunch. My stepfather's approach to shopping also meant we bought just seven pieces of fruit for each family member every week. If a friend came over and ate one of my bananas, I was out the next day. If she ate one of my mom's Granny Smith apples, that meant a hike to the grocery store to replace it.

Now, as a mom who is tortured by massive food waste on a daily basis, I see the beauty in my stepfather's approach—yet surely there has to be a happy medium. Perhaps my kids will get it right in their own adulthood.

6:30–8:00   Finish homework and talk on the phone.

8:00–9:00   TV.

9:00   In bed, usually asleep by 9:30 if not sooner.

Wednesday nights had me at choir practice from 6 to 9 p.m., meaning it was a hustle to shower, grab something to eat, and get my butt in the choir room right after practice. I was pushing myself mentally from 7:30 a.m. to 2 p.m. and then physically from 3 p.m. to 9 p.m., surrounded by people I really liked, and I fell asleep exhausted but happy.

Weekends were full of cross-country and track meets, hanging out in basements with my friends, being silly, reading, and taking long walks around the neighborhood pondering life.

Why am I telling you all of this?

Because if I flash back to that Eddie moment, where I know I was feeling really good overall, I can go back in time and see all the things that made me feel alive. It allows me to examine the things that were going right. I had a regular wake-up time and routine. It was so regimented (6:03 a.m.—I can still see the alarm clock if I close my eyes) that I didn't know how not to do it. Our cross-country and track workouts were beyond challenging, with two-mile warm-ups and two-mile cooldowns, and some sort of ridiculousness in between. I had a creative outlet (choir). I saw friends regularly. I got amazing sleep and had a set bedtime. I even went to bed relatively early on the weekends. (The curse of a 10 p.m. curfew.)

In review, I can see why 1997 was one of my best years. I was seventeen. It was the first time in my childhood years that I had freedom. So long as my chores were done, I was left alone. I had free rein to do the things I wanted to do and go where I wanted to go, so long as I came home in time for dinner. When I was with my friends and fellow runners, I had free rein to be me.

Before that, everything had been a slog. Elementary school was a social nightmare. I attended three different elementary schools in the span of three years. In third grade, I was the weird new kid from Scotland. Fourth grade, my parents changed my school due to bullying. In fifth grade, my parents' divorce was finalized and my mom remarried, so we moved a few neighborhoods over. Then, in sixth grade, I was the new kid again when I moved to my stepfather's home. If you are counting, that is four schools and four peer groups within a span of five years.

My middle school experience was probably like most—I was bullied, I was called names, I was misunderstood, I wasn't in the right classes. It took me until eighth grade to find a "group," and even then, I never actually felt like I fit in and never felt cool enough to be in the "cool kids' group" I ached to be a part of.

Life didn't "click" until tenth grade, when our friend group finally discovered one another. Each of us fit, and each of us had a place in the puzzle. We loved each other fiercely and truly. At the same time, I was finding my footing in leadership and was on my way to becoming a young captain of my running teams.

When Eddie, said those words to me in the hallway, it was one of the first times I felt like someone saw me and liked me for who I was, deep on the inside. More importantly, someone saw the "me" I had yearned to be for so many years. The person who I had felt had gone missing during my parents' divorce. Eddie's words were a sparkle put on my path.

Why wasn't college my magical time? As you will read in chapter 9, I got whammied with so many self-limiting beliefs during that time that I began a new spiral of self-doubt that lasted for over a decade.

The same can be said for my three years in law school.

After that? I think we are all familiar with the race to find a job, get engaged, buy a home, get married, and have babies. We are so busy trying to achieve the next thing or reach the next milestone that we spend little to no time actually tuning in and asking ourselves, "What really feels like 'me'?"

When Was Your Best Version of You?

I want you to sit back, close your eyes, and take a breath in and a breath out. We are going to go on a journey to see if we can remember *when* you felt the most like you. Let's travel to a time before you had all of the pressure of college, grad school, job searches, partner searches, and fertility journeys. I am not saying all of your journeys haven't contributed to the amazing, weathered, insightful, and strong person you have become. Not at all. I know full well that all of those experiences you had in your adult life have shaped you to be the professional and parent you are. Yet it still matters that we go back and remember you as a person on the inside, before you were driven by all of those external forces.

Travel back to a time where you can remember feeling "carefree." What did you do just for the fun of it? Was there a time when you felt true happiness? Maybe in your memory you are in your backyard, swinging on a huge tire. Maybe you are riding your bike around the neighborhood, meandering down roads you had never seen before. Maybe you are sitting on the floor of your bedroom, drawing. Maybe you are driving home from practice with a new driver's license, and you take the scenic route home just because you can, with all of the windows down and the AC on, just like your mom never let you, but that day, you knew it would feel glorious. Maybe you just got home from hanging out with the new girl at school and, for the first time in a long time, you found that someone "got" you. Maybe your mom just took you to visit a big city and see a show for the first time. Maybe you are just wandering your neighborhood, searching for creeks to wade in, with just a watch and a reminder to be home in time for dinner. Note, this does not have to be a search for a happy childhood memory (maybe there aren't any). This can be a search for the first time you felt true freedom. What was happening in that moment?

Deep breathe, in and out.

Now I want you to imagine your now-adult self, talking to this younger or freer version of you. Imagine yourself sitting next to her, cross-legged on her bedroom floor with your backs leaning on the bed, as you say to her, "It's your call on how we spend the day. What do you want to do?" What does she say? How does she want to spend her time?

If she isn't sure, see how she feels about going on an adventure; baking something new and delicious; playing her favorite sport; lying in her bed and listening to music; getting together with friends from down the street; going to a concert; buying new art supplies; going to the movies; shopping; hiking. Which idea did she love? Which idea provoked a memory that made her (and you) smile? What made her jump up and say, "That sounds fun! Let's go"?

Now imagine her doing the activity. While she is in it, who is she surrounded by? What is she thinking about? What fills her cup? What annoys the crap out of her? What does she get excited about? Who does she want to spend her time with the most? Doing what? Is she babbling away at you, telling you everything? Is she tight-lipped and nervous about what she might say? If so, can you look into her eyes and remember what is going on in her brain? What is she thinking but too afraid to say out loud?

GRIT-work

Get out your **GRIT-workbook!**

In this section, I want you to pick one thing that really lit your fire at some point in your past.

That one thing that lit your fire? We need to add that back in to your life. Stat. This will be what helps to end your Groundhog Day cycle. In the workbook, answer the following prompts:

1) What was the one thing that made you feel like *you*? Did it bring you joy?
2) What is the adult version of that one thing? Can you add it back in to your life?
3) Do you commit to making it a part of your life? How? When? Where?
4) What are three action steps you can take to make this happen?

Note: If you have just finished this section and are coming up blank, I want you to go back on a treasure hunt one more time. Even if you find something small and tiny and seemingly insignificant, I want you to envision what life would be like if you invited the adult version of that thing back into your life today.

If you are still feeling empty, we need to do this exercise on the inverse. When you go back in time, is there something that bugged you about your life as a kid that still bugs you today? Great—we are getting somewhere. It's time to purge. Name three action steps to help you purge and get going on them (now).

Ideal World

This is the time to dream and think big. I want you to picture what life would look like in an ideal world three years from now. Imagine if you could teleport in time again, this time into the future à la Marty McFly in *Back to the Future Part II*, and you are living the life of your dreams. (If you are a *Back to the Future* fan like I am, think about it from Marty's point of view once everything is "fixed" at the end of the movie, as opposed to in the beginning when he is living a nightmare!)

GRIT-work

Take the time (yes, we are doing this right now!). Set a timer for ten minutes so that you can focus on being fully present. Start by sitting back in your chair. Deep breathe, in and out. We are flying forward into time, three years from now. You are watching your future self go about her day, walking around her house, working, talking to the kids, and talking to herself in the mirror. Imagine yourself tagging along with her all day long, watching what she does and how she talks, and getting to peek into her thoughts. Throughout the day, you make observations of her and celebrate her. What do you see?

Write it all down.

If you need more particulars:

What time do you wake up?

What are you doing in the morning?

How do you get ready for the day?

What are you wearing?

What do you eat for lunch? Where?

How do you spend your afternoon?

Your evenings?

Who are you with throughout the day?

Are you working? What are you doing? Are you at the same job? Have you started a new one?

Who are you surrounded by on a daily basis?

What are you doing for fun?

Is it something else?

What have you finally gotten rid of?

Breathe in and out. Spend some time here relishing in the most ideal world that you are living in.

Write it all down.

Now, even though this version of life has not yet occurred, I want you to take a minute and give so much gratitude for this future life. I want you to feel the smile spread across your lips as you feel yourself in this world you have created. I want you to see yourself surrounded by love. Laughing. Content. Let any worries that this "might not be real" or "will never actually happen" slip and melt away. Bask in the contentment.

Breathe in and out.

Putting It All Together

So often, we get stuck in a rut. Over time, the rut grows so deep and the walls seem so tall that we find it easier to stay put, doing the same thing over and over, even though we no longer derive any joy from it. The reason why? (We cover this more in chapter 11.) Our brain's job is to keep us safe. Our nervous system is trying to protect us from the harm of the unknown. Our brain has decided that the "old" way of doing things hasn't killed us yet, so it might as well keep doing that same thing over and over again. Have you heard the saying, "What doesn't kill you will make you stronger"? Au contraire when it comes to the brain—what doesn't kill you will keep you safe and stagnant.

Here is a mind-bender: the brain, the part of our bodies that *thinks* for us, does not always know best.

Don't believe me? There is a really neat website, Akiyoshi's illusion pages, created by Professor Akiyoshi Kitaoka, a researcher at the Ritsumeikan University in Japan. I invite you to take a few minutes and visit it: https://www.ritsumei.ac.jp/~akitaoka/index-e.html. Aren't all of those illustrations wild? While we are well aware that the images aren't actually moving, our brains believe they are. Do you see how easily our brains can be tricked?

If our brains can play tricks on us this easily, can you see how our brains can also play tricks on us to keep us "safe" but stagnant? Is *safe* what is *best* for your growth as a human? As a mom? As a professional? Is "safe" protecting you? Or is it actually holding you back?

Consider the following quote from writer Courtney C. Stevens: "If nothing changes, nothing changes. If you keep doing what you're doing, you're going to keep getting what you're getting. You want change, make some." What are you ready to change?

GRIT-work

We did our GRIT-work early in this chapter. This is your gentle (but firm!) reminder to make sure you complete it. I also have one more worksheet for you in the GRIT-workbook. Crack it open and get down to business.

1) After doing the exercises and mind journeys into the best *you* you can remember, what really lit your fire back then? What brought you the *most* joy?
2) Do you hereby commit to adding this one thing back into your life stat?

3) Fill out the pledge in the **GRIT-workbook**: I,_____,
hereby COMMIT to adding_____ back into
my life. I will do this by _____ [DATE].
4) List three action steps to make it happen.

CHAPTER 5

Find Your Anchor: The Secrets behind a Killer Morning Routine

"Beautiful Day," U2

On Your Mark

It's time to roll up our sleeves—or roll down the covers—and get to work. Creating a morning routine is key to a life of sparkle & GRIT. Before we go further, let's have a quick chat on *why* a morning routine is essential. I am guessing that if you're in my network already, one of the reasons you are reading this book is because you see me living my morning routine every morning and you are craving the same. Why is it crucial? Because a morning routine is key to us living our best technicolor lives. In the words of Hal Elrod from *Miracle Morning*:

> *How you wake up each day and your morning routine (or lack thereof) dramatically affects your levels of success in every single area of your life. Focused, productive, successful mornings generate focused, productive, successful days—which inevitably create a successful*

life—in the same way that unfocused, unproductive, and mediocre mornings generate unfocused, unproductive, and mediocre days, and ultimately a mediocre quality of life. By simply changing the way you wake up in the morning, you can transform any area of your life, faster than you ever thought possible.[7]

I am living proof of this concept and the internal metamorphosis it inspires. I did not always have a morning routine, and I vividly remember how lethargic, foggy, blah, and, in Hal's words, mediocre, I felt. In my gut, I knew that creating a morning routine would be a lifeline. Once I finally got over the hump of just starting, life began to transform before my eyes. Ever since I began creating and following a morning routine that works for me, I wake up with a fire and I am more productive, creative, and focused than I have ever been. When I start to stray away from a morning routine, I become unfocused and increasingly more anxious.

Not surprisingly, creating a morning routine comes up in every single one-to-one life coaching session I have. It is probably the *most* requested and effective tool to help my clients get unstuck, find their passion, and begin to really discover who they are again.

Do I have your buy-in yet?

Before you panic, we are going to go slow. I don't expect you to wake up super early tomorrow, meditate, journal, read, advance the laundry, hit the gym, meal prep, and do all of the things, but we are going to start the **GRIT-work** early in this chapter.

---

7. Hal Elrod, The Miracle Morning: The Not-So-Obvious Secret Guaranteed to Transform your Life Before 8AM (New York: Hal Elrod International, 2016), 3.

To begin, let's start with what you have now and what is working or not working.

GRIT-workbook

Find your **GRIT-workbook** and answer the prompts that serve you best:

1) I have a "morning routine," and I can tell it to you down to the minute. Here it is:
2) There are some parts of my morning routine that I really like (such as _____), but I would like to add the following:
3) I am so lost. I know I need some sort of morning routine. If I could magically add three things, they would be these three:

Now I want you to rate yourself on a scale of 1 to 10 (10 being "I am a freaking rock star" and 1 being a big old "WELP") on the following GRITTY Activities Essential to a Morning Routine:

- I wake up at the same time every day.
- I wake up before my kids.
- I am good at not pressing the snooze button on my phone/alarm.
- I ignore social media until later in the day.
- I start each day with a big cup of water.
- I spend some time journaling.
- I spend some quiet time with my coffee/tea/matcha/hot water.
- I move/intentionally break a sweat.
- I spend at least five minutes in meditation.
- I map out the three things I need to get done that day.
- I have a set bedtime and turn off my electronics an hour beforehand.
- I go to bed before 11 p.m.

Awesome. Thank you for doing that. We will come back to your answers in a bit.

Get Set
(Wake Up Before the Kids)

Now is the best time to tell you that you are never going to be 100% "ready" to start your new shiny morning routine. There will always be something in the way—a late night, a sick kid, a crappy night's sleep, a big day ahead. Stop letting all of that get in the way. This is your sign—it is time!

If you only get one takeaway from this entire book, please let it be this one: it is imperative that you wake up before your kids. If you are waking up to a crying toddler, an adventurous six-year-old tapping you on your head who is ready to break out the LEGO and Play-Doh at an ungodly hour, or, my personal current fave, your tween screaming for you—"MOOOOOOOOOOOM!!!!!"—like she is about to get into a fight with someone, you have already started your day behind the eight ball.

For my mamas with newborns who are not sleeping through the night and need every golden drop of Zz's you can get, please feel free to ignore this part and come back to it when you are ready and have the capacity. Bookmark it, sticky note it, just please, once your little one is finally getting in decent stretches of sleep (and you are too), come back!

When you wake up before the kids, you create the time to have an uninterrupted thought. It is the one moment, in all of your twenty-four hours, when you are not "on," when no one is asking anything of you and the day is brand spanking new. It is *the* best time for you to take a moment for yourself.

If you are thinking, *Well, hmm, I don't wanna wake up before I have to, so I am going to flip this advice around and, instead of waking up before the kids, I will just get my 'me time' in once the kids are asleep . . .*

That doesn't count.

We aren't looking for "me time." We are giving you a moment to *be* before your day starts. For so many of my clients, "me time" involves social media scrolling, Netflix, cleaning up the kitchen, responding to work emails, and drinking wine.

This is not what we are going for here.

Even if you are fighting me and telling me that you *promise* that you will use the end of the day for "good," remember what we learned about willpower. By the end of the day, your willpower is running on empty. Your brain isn't fresh, and instead, it is likely fried from all the things that happened over the day, because likely so *much* has happened since the morning.

Let's take a little glimpse, shall we?

I am betting that a usual day begins with a kid hollering for you to come into their room. You walk in and, immediately, he begins complaining about a runny nose and headache. For a minute, you freak out that he is for-real sick (thanks, COVID) and start worrying about how you are going to stay home with him. Your brain is going a mile a minute, rearranging your whole day. Then, five minutes later, you are relieved to see that he is okay and can in fact go to school. Yet that doesn't stop the smattering of worry about whether you are making the right decision. In all of that muck, the time you had set aside to pack your lunch went out the window, and now you are running around the kitchen cobbling together breakfasts and kid lunches, and you smack your head into an open cabinet, and a large welt is starting to grow on the side of your head, and it *hurts*, goshdammit! Then, as soon as the kiddos are on the bus, you open up your email to find a nasty email from a coworker, or from your boss, or, for my law moms out there, from opposing counsel. *Grrr.* Traffic is awful and you hit every red light, making you late. You walk into your office, annoyed and not wanting to make eye contact with anyone for fear of really losing it or breaking down. Once you scroll through the easier emails, you fire off a response to the nasty email, leaving you feeling aggravated and tired, yet simultaneously vindicated. Instead of getting back into your work projects, you go over to IG and scroll through anonymous happy smiling people who all seem to have it more together than you do. Forty-five minutes have disappeared in a flash. You only become aware of the time when you get interrupted by an incoming call from the school letting you know that your kiddo forgot the cobbled-together lunch and they need confirmation that yes, your child can buy today (why is this even a phone call?). Now you are running late to your dentist appointment, where you find out that all of your nighttime teeth grinding has cracked a tooth and you need a crown, which will cost $800—great. You treat yourself to a "fun" Starbucks drink on the way back to the office, but it ends up tasting gross because you are pretty sure they used real milk and not the oat milk you requested. Another $8 down the drain (and when did these drinks start costing the same amount as a burrito?!). It is only 12:45 p.m. . . .

Need I go further?

. . . Okay, let's keep going. I need to drive this point home because we both know I am painting a picture of a legit, real day in your life (mine too).

On your drive back to the office, you call your father to check in. He immediately launches into a story about his own day and how it was pretty grueling because of the long line at the post office. This conversation prompts you to remember, oh *crap!!* You *still* have not mailed your Aunt Marsha's Christmas present to her (and it is now April). Once you get back to the office, you *finally* sit down to start the project that has been bugging you all day, but then you are pulled out of it only a few minutes in because it is time to sing "Happy Birthday" to Carol down the hall. You scoot out right at 5, swing by the house to drop off your car and combine forces with your partner, pick up the kids from aftercare, and throw them something to eat on the way to gymnastics. Once you are finally home, you might attempt to make a more real second dinner, and then it is time to get the kids to bed.

How close am I?

How on *earth* do you have anything left in the tank after a day like that, a day full of uncontrollables? While this book will help you streamline your days and make it easier for you to balance the scales of work and life, the reality is that being a full-time mom and a full-time professional and a full-time adult equates to a lot of "stuff" that is unavoidable. A lot of stuff that drains us. How can we *not* feel comatose at the end of the day?

And do you see how, at the end of the day, your brain isn't even really yours anymore? When you give yourself a fighting chance and plug into you *before* all of that nonsense (and it is so much nonsense), you are gifting yourself the very best and freshest part of you, with a rested, clean brain that actually has time to think.

That is why you must wake up before the kids.

In the following sections, I am going to talk about anchors and encourage you to adopt one of them ASAP so you can start creating your own morning routine, but if you need to start slow, I want you to spend two weeks simply waking up before the kids. All you have to do is wake up. I am not even asking you to do anything else. Just get up, have a cup of coffee or tea in silence (no scrolling social media or watching crap television or the news), and take that moment. In silence. Alone.

Awesome. Great start. Do it for two weeks.

Go!

Now that we are waking up before our kids, it is time to find our first anchor. Here, an anchor is that one thing you will commit to doing every morning. An anchor comes in the form of GRITTY action and something you must *do*. Over time, this one anchor will serve as a lifeline and will become such a part of you that you will not know how *not* to do it anymore (like brushing your teeth!). Once your anchor is in place, it will be easier to add in other anchors. Building your morning routine one GRITTY step at a time is the secret sauce to crafting a morning routine you stick with.

In the following sections, I share with you all of the very best anchors. These are anchors that work. Read through them and see which anchor resonates with you the most. Take notes. By the end of this chapter, you will commit to one of these anchors, so as you read, think about which one you might be most interested in committing to (this week!).

I know—you are worried this is going to be a drag. You are worried about losing sleep. You are worried about having to give up the warm comfort of your bed. Flip it. Instead, be worried about what you are missing out on when you don't have that quiet time before your kids wake up. Be nervous about what happens if you don't use this sacred time when your "willpower" is fully gassed up. Instead of mourning your bed, celebrate *you!*

Anchor 1: Sweat

My first anchor? *Sweat*. Brought to me in the form of an amazing gentleman named Shaun T. Shaun T often says, "If you can hold up your body, you can hold up your life," and I couldn't agree more. Let's talk about how I learned the truth of that statement.

I already told you a little bit about how everything changed for me in the summer of 2015. Before that point, I had *thought* a lot about working out again, resurrecting runner Wendy. For years, I had hemmed and hawed, trying to decide whether I was ready to be a worker-outer again and debating what kind of workout to choose. I googled the workouts I saw on infomercials and would get as far as the checkout page. I put DVDs in my Amazon cart and read a billion reviews. Each time I was ready to check out, I bailed. Everything seemed too hard, too time-intensive, and too expensive. I was not ready to invest $100 on DVDs that I feared would just sit on the shelf and get dusty. Back in 2015, I didn't trust myself enough to spend that kind of money on myself. It felt decadent and a little selfish.

Then, one afternoon, my law partner dropped into my office and said, "Wen! I just got a copy of T25! Do you think we should do it?" The sparkle in his eye was infectious. I didn't want to say no. T25, a DVD workout series that promised to get you into shape in just twenty-five minutes a day, had always been a contender and had graced my shopping cart at least a dozen times. How could I say no to the chance to have someone else doing it at the same time as me, especially when it was only twenty-five minutes a day? I didn't know what I was really getting into, but I had to say yes. It was time for me to invest in myself.

But then my law partner dropped a bomb and had the audacity to show me the workout calendar we had to follow. My stomach plummeted. "You mean we can't just pick and choose? That is what I normally do. I love doing arms and abs."

"No. This is the calendar, and we mark it off as we go."

"Oh."

I did my best to hide my terror. Yet I felt this stirring. I felt possibility. I felt butterflies. We picked a start date and, as cliché as I know this sounds, the rest really was history.

The next Monday morning, and every morning thereafter for two solid months, my alarm would go off at 6 on the dot. I was downstairs in my kitchen by 6:05, shoes laced. I pulled up T25 on an old laptop and went to work, right there in the middle of the kitchen, volume low so I would not wake up the whole house. Twenty-five minutes of straight sweat. I dreaded it and loved it at the same time. A few hours later, my former law partner and I would roll into the office and say things like "Can you believe those one-arm burpees!" or "Thank goodness he let us take a minute to stretch today" or "My calves are burning!" Sweating with Shaun T and feeling like a badass every morning had me feeling downright giddy.

The fact that I showed up every day for ten weeks straight amazed me. I could not believe I showed up that consistently for that long. Even when I was on vacation. Even when I had a work trip. Even when I did the workout on the second-floor landing of my mother- and father-in-law's beach house, looking over the rest of the family relaxing in the living room. I completed every darn day of that calendar for almost three months straight!

It hurt at first. I would try not to look at the countdown clock for as long as I could. After a few weeks of the routine, though, I noticed a happy, bubbly Wendy emerging. My brain started to work faster, and the fog and cobwebs began to clear. I felt more energetic. I started bouncing into work. I started to run around more with the kids. I felt tuned into the happy, bubbly, running Wendy from 1997.

So often you hear people say, "I found me again" or "I found myself." *This* is what that means. When you find that past self you are most proud of and feel her come back to life. I finally had the anchor I needed to start my morning routine. I finally had a *reason* to wake up early. I had a GRITTY step and, because I took it each day, my sparkle grew brighter and brighter. She opened more possibilities.

My anchor of sweat buoyed the base of my morning routine.

Take a minute and think about using sweat as your anchor. Did any part of my story resonate with you? Do you remember a young woman or girl who, once upon a time, was physically active? Or maybe it was a you from your twenties or thirties, when you first discovered your love of running or playing tennis or swimming? Do you remember how you *felt* when you were in your sparkling, glowy, sweaty (GRITTY) glory? What else was working for you back then? Did working out allow other doors to open for you? Did you make new connections? Find new friends? Think about your job differently? What did sweat do for you before? Are you ready to welcome in sweat again to be your anchor?

One more thing to think about before we go to the next anchor. While sweat was my action item anchor and what made me feel downright amazing, accountability was key as well. Knowing my law partner was also pressing play every morning added motivation to keep going on. The solidarity and not wanting to let him down by failing to do a workout are what propelled me to get out of bed on the mornings I really did not want to. My former law partner doesn't know this, but I am forever grateful for that pocket of time. It changed my life. It was the key to the door that I didn't know I needed to unlock. If having accountability resonates with you, find your partner in crime!

Anchor 2: Read

There is a really neat thing that happens to our brains when we read. In general, the simple act of reading not only increases our intelligence, but it leads to a higher-functioning and healthier brain.[8] Not only that, but reading also reduces our stress and improves our memory and concentration.[9] With brain fog setting in as we leave our thirties and enter our forties, aren't these benefits enough to get you to run to your local library and carve out time every day to get in your daily reading prescription?

Another fact I find really interesting? When we read a story, our brains are interpreting it as if we are actually in the story and experiencing it.[10] This is why reading can feel so real and palpable to us. Why we can cry, laugh, and sometimes have that "just woke up from a dream" feeling when we are truly immersed in a book.

This is the same for books that I call "personal development." You might know them as "self-help books" or books on leadership. Just as we can lose ourselves in a story and feel like we are there living it as if we are the main character, the same is true with personal development. In these cases, it is as if the author is speaking directly to you and is a voice inside your head. Just like this book. Because of this peculiar sort of quantum travel, it feels like you are actually being coached by the author. Because of this unique bond between author/coach and

---

8. Lia Tabackman, "5 Ways Reading Benefits Your Health—And How to Make Reading a Daily Habit," Insider, December 1, 2020, https://www.insider.com/guides/health/benefits-of-reading.

9. Tabackman, "5 Ways Reading Benefits Your Health."

10. "Your Brain on Books: 10 Things That Happen to Our Minds When We Read," Open Education Database, accessed July 13, 2023, https://oedb.org/ilibrarian/your-brain-on-books-10-things-that-happen-to-our-minds-when-we-read/.

reader/student, it is possible to reap many of the benefits of one-to-one coaching, even though we are not physically in the same space, nor exchanging spoken words. This is what is also allowing you, my reader, to feel like we are working together in this book, why we have made a connection, why you are letting yourself be coachable—because it is you and me, right here right now.

I know that you are afraid that this sort of reading might be boring. That you aren't in learning mode. You may feel that you would rather read fluff because your brain is just too tired to take in any more. I was in the same place—until I wasn't. I didn't understand the power of "self-help" books either, but I knew something was missing, and I figured I would give it a shot. I didn't want to "waste" my morning time reading, so instead, I downloaded a couple books off of Audible and figured I could at least try this personal development thing during my commute to and from work. And so my obsession with nonfiction began—and so, too, began my book-buying addiction. Know this: these books have a funny way of grabbing you with a passage or a line. That line will sit a little uncomfortably. You will go back and read it. You will rewind and listen again. You will feel raw and awake, all at once. Then you will notice that one line pops up as a theme everywhere else until you can ignore it no longer.

My line?

I can tell you exactly where I was when I heard it. Like I said, I was still courting the idea of this thing called personal development, and I only made time for it on my commute. One morning, I was at a stoplight, right in front of the local Royal Farms. It was May 2018, and I didn't know yet that my family's whole life was about to change, but there was this one line that grabbed me and shook me to my core:

"Nobody is going to help you achieve it. Not really. *You* have to decide to pursue your wildest dreams." (From Rachel Hollis's *Girl, Wash Your Face*; emphasis added.)

This line came just after Rach reminded us that nobody else on this planet will care about our dreams as much as we do:

> *Even if you have a supportive family. Even if you have*
> *the greatest friends alive. Even if your spouse is the*
> *most uplifting, encouraging human and your number*
> *one fan . . . even then, girl, they will not want it as much*
> *as you do. It doesn't keep them up at night. It doesn't*
> *light their soul on fire. It's your dream.*

Once I heard that quote, I could not unhear it. I hadn't realized that I had been sitting around waiting for someone else to make my dream happen. Rach's writing woke me up. She gave me the courage and direction that the "something" that was going to change my life could only be one thing: me.

Then, just a few weeks later, a (really) big change happened. On the Saturday of Memorial Day weekend, my stepfather, Al, was cycling, helmet on and in the cyclist lane, and was hit by a motorist. By Sunday, we learned he was brain-dead, and my family quickly honored his very well-known wishes and took him off life support. That weekend, and the weeks of grief thereafter, were god-awful. Once the initial wave of shock and grief began to lift, that line about following my dreams began to haunt me. My stepfather had been a true Renaissance man and had never stopped following or working for his dreams. In his career, he had been a wildly passionate scientist, thrilled to do work as a civil servant for NIH. In his health, he had overcome his asthma and qualified for the Boston Marathon multiple times over. In his later years, his dogged determination had empowered him to become a certified botanical illustrator, no matter how many setbacks and frustrations he faced along the way. I cannot remember a period of time when he wasn't not only following, but going *all in*, on one of his dreams. He did exactly what he wanted to do at all times, unapologetically.

If he could do it, why couldn't I?

As I woke up from the grief, and as family and friends discussed Al's memory, that one line kept lurking: "Nobody is going to help you achieve it." Al didn't sit around waiting for his dreams to be handed to him. He went after them with dogged determination, and he didn't stop until he got what he wanted.

I could not hide anymore. It was time to make a change.

Check out this timeline. May 2018, I heard Hollis's words. August 2018, I opened the doors to my own firm.

This is what these books do. They grab you. They wake you up. They lodge ideas into your brain, ideas you can't let go of. As we start to fill our minds with words from mentors (because that is what these authors truly are—mentors, nudging us along), our lives begin to change in the most beautiful ways. Our confidence starts to increase. We become motivated to try something new. We start to walk with a spring to our step because of some newfound inspiration that we didn't have before.

Knowing all of that, can you see how spending just ten minutes or ten pages of reading personal development first thing in the morning can help nudge you along on this journey? If you aren't ready to spend your precious morning time on this quite yet, can you commit to listening to something in the car?

Anchor 3: Journaling

When I mention journaling to my clients and colleagues, I usually hear, "Who has time for that?! I don't want to write a diary!" or, "That sounds arduous," or, "I don't want to write all of my thoughts and feelings out—that sounds too overwhelming."

What if I told you that, in my kind of journal, you don't have to spend any time freehanding all of your feelings and emotions or giving blow-by-blows of your days, and you don't have to spend time digging into your past childhood self? What if I told you that you could spend about seven minutes, get in and get out, and have a (*way*) better day as a result? Would you consider it then?

In this section, I am going to introduce you to my absolute favorite journaling prompts, which allow me to live a life full of sparkle & GRIT. If these inspire you, I encourage you to dedicate a spiral notebook to journaling and focus on what I discuss in this anchor: affirmations, gratitude, and concrete ways to plug into your family.[11] Simply focusing on a few key items and getting in and getting out is the most efficient and motivating way to nail down this anchor.

Journaling—Affirmations

The best part about journaling? It is the most effective tool to ensure you show up as the person you want to be, all with a quick scan of the day ahead, an "I am" statement, and a short visualization.

How does it work? Each morning, give yourself the opportunity and space to examine your day before it happens. As you scan ahead,

---

11. I actually have a sparkle & GRIT journal available if you are ready to pick journaling as your anchor and want to see a lot of what I talk about here laid out in a fun and pleasing way – a perfect way to start your day! Visit the sparkle & GRIT resources page to find out more.

figure out which event or task is going to require the most of you. From there, figure out "who" you want to show up as to said event/task so that it runs as smoothly as possible. As you think about the who, you can then come up with an "I am" statement that will support you all day long. This works because when we write down something as if it has already happened—or, in this instance, we write down *who* we are as a person as if we are already that person—our brain already believes that this is the case. This works even better if you give yourself a moment, breathe in, breathe out, and repeat the "I am" statement as you visualize yourself in the moment, acting as if you already are that person as you do so.

Here are my favorite ways that affirmations have shown up in my life and how they 100% made a difference.

"I am unwavering."

It was the morning of trial. My client was a mom seeking custody of her teenage daughter and let's just say that her baby daddy was a (major) piece of work. I had a "zesty" piece of evidence that I was dying to have admitted by the judge because it got to the heart of the father's off-putting and misogynistic character in one fell swoop. I knew that the father's lawyer would object. I also knew that the evidence's relevance was not obvious at first glance. But getting in this document mattered to me (and my client) so that the judge would know just who this guy really was.

That morning, I wrote in my journal, "I am calm, but a force." Later that morning, on my commute to work, I also decided that I would be "unwavering."

Several hours later—it was go time—I was in the middle of my cross-examination and ready to present these rather juicy documents. From opposing counsel: "Objection! Relevancy."

The judge gave me the opportunity to be heard, and I stated my case as I had rehearsed already.

"Overruled." (Meaning I had another go at it.)

I approached the witness with the same paper, continuing on with my questions and ready to really go after this guy.

Another "Objection!" stopped me in my tracks. Opposing counsel had some more *blah blah blah* and a new relevancy argument.

Again, I argued why this piece of evidence was important, increasing my zeal and becoming more animated.

"Overruled."

Yes! I was going to get it in! I tried again and for a third time.

"Objection!" (*Oh my word, when would this man just let me get in my damn piece of evidence?!*)

Now, if this had been a Wendy who had *not* set an affirmation to be "calm," "a force," and "unwavering," I would have backed down and whispered to my client, "I am so sorry, we aren't going to be able to get this evidence in. He keeps objecting, and this is not going to end up going our way. We are wasting our time, and we just need to move on."

But—I had journaled that morning.

This time, this third damn time, like a broken record on triple speed, I passionately and feistily argued my position—again. With even more force and particularity, I explained (again) why this document and line of questioning were relevant and why it would be important for the judge to consider it in her ruling.

Judge: "Overruled—it is admitted."

Yes!

And the trial went on.

Now, when I know I have a difficult task coming up, I conjure up the affirmation, "I am unwavering."

"I am a loving wife."

Journal affirmations aren't just about how we show up at work. They can be used to describe how we show up as a spouse or partner.

One Friday a few summers ago, my husband was leaving for a boys' trip to Ocean City, Maryland. My day was packed with calls and drafting agreements, meaning it would be hard for me to tear myself away from the computer, even for a few minutes. But, when I wrote in my journal that morning, I decided I would be a "loving wife" that day. When I closed my eyes to consider what that would mean and look like, I figured out that it would be "to really, truly hug Kirk goodbye and lean into the hug."

A few hours later, he was coming down the stairs to leave. I was sitting there, typing away, on a break between Zooms. My knee-jerk reaction? To wait for him to come to me, then barely tear my eyes from the screen, give him a quick peck, and send him on his way. But instead, I remembered what I had written and planned for. As he was coming down the stairs, I got up out of my chair and walked out of the office. I followed him into the hallway and reached for a hug. And I didn't let go. I stayed in the hug and leaned the weight of my whole entire body onto him. I was so 100% present in that hug that I can still *feel* it years later.

In that moment, not only did I show up as 100% the wife I wanted to be, but I created a memory, a palpable one, that I get to keep for the rest of my life. How wild is that?

"I am not a yelling mommy."

I cannot tell you how many times I have used this one. I remember reading a passage in *Girl, Wash Your Face* where Rach was describing a time that she yelled so hard at her kids that her teeth rattled. I recall thinking, *Gosh, I know I am a yeller, but I don't know if I have ever yelled like that.*

91

Until the time I did.

Usually, the crazy yelling mommy Wendy reared her head when I was trying to get the kids out the door and make it to the bus on time. Without fail, every morning when it is time to leave, I look down at my kids and one doesn't have socks and the other needs to poop. I start to get stressed about the time, feeling my thoughts go a mile a minute—"Why on earth does he not have socks? We talked about this thirty minutes ago! And why on earth does she need to poop *now* when she has been up for like three hours? Really?!" I start to seethe inside. I start to get worried about missing the bus. The kids' level of distress at this situation does not nearly match mine, which just makes me more mad that *they have no flipping clue or care that we are about to miss the bus! If we miss the bus, I need to drive them to school! If I need to do that, I will be late to my meeting! Why does no one care?!* As I start to cajole them into doing what they need to do, my voice starts to rise and I start to snap my fingers at them. One is still upstairs getting socks. The other is still stuck in the bathroom. I start to *roar!*

"What is happening?! Are you freaking kidding me?! We need to get going and need to get into the car *now!!*"

Finally, we are in the car on the way to the bus stop. But for some reason, I don't stop yelling. Instead, I think it is a "good" idea for the kids to really know and understand how mad I am. What do I do? I yell more. They start crying, looking at each other for comfort.

Fuck.

And all of this is minutes before I will be putting them on the bus (because, yes, we are still somehow always miraculously on time).

But I am looking at their little faces, at the tears streaming down their cheeks. Wondering, *How the eff did I get here? What am I doing?* This is awful. This is not the mommy I want to be. My teeth feel rattled—oh.

I get them both out of the car to wait for the bus. I hug them so hard. I promise I will do better. I explain that, while Mommy was frustrated, she was out of line.

I still feel like shit.

Yelling comes naturally to me. I was raised by a grade-ten yeller and was raised to yell back. When my husband asked for my hand in marriage (the poor man decided to ask both my dad and stepdad), do you know what my stepdad's response was? "Do you know how to fight? Promise me that you will fight." He was well-meaning. His biggest fear (for any marriage) was that a couple would sweep their problems under the rug, which would grow to resentment, which would grow to separation, which would grow to divorce.

My husband and me? Sure, we yell sometimes. About once a year, we yell like crazy people and go a little nutty, giving each other a middle-finger dance, which *usually* makes one of us laugh. Then, once it is all out, we talk rationally, move on, and, within minutes, we are having a normal conversation about who is getting the kids off the bus this week or where we should go next weekend for dinner. We are able to reset *fast*.

But the same does not apply to the kiddos.

And I should fully know this because, while I was raised in a yelling household and while yelling was the norm for me, I hated being yelled at. It made me feel less than. It made me feel small. I hated the feeling of fights that ended with me retreating to my room, crying under the covers, and feeling emotionally beaten up, ultimately resolving into nothing other than the feeling that I had to submit.

Then why, oh why, do I yell so hard at them—ever? Why do I do the same damn thing?

Looking back and unpacking it? My default when stressed is to yell. My emotional circuits have been hardwired one way, and now I am actively doing the hard work to reroute them.

Also, perhaps if I *myself* weren't also running behind each morning, it all would go a little smoother. *This* is the kicker, folks. If I got myself together even ten minutes sooner, crisis would be averted. Hmm. Think about that a bit. How often do we as moms get so annoyed with ourselves that we take our frustration out on everyone else around us? Since that realization, I have begun journaling "I am not a yelling mommy" on the mornings I know I will need that added reminder.

When I use this affirmation, it reminds me to also have my own shit together and be in a good place to herd the kids out the door. It also reminds me that when all hell breaks loose, as will happen when you have littles that I am not in fact a yelling mommy. It nudges me all day long to take a breath and think before I start to raise my voice. That mantra sits in the back of my brain, poking me and reminding me that yelling the kids into submission serves only one purpose: to make my family feel like shit. It stops me mid-yell. When I feel my voice increasing in decibels, I make a conscious effort to just stop, pause, breathe, and think about the mom I want to be.

Once we can stop yelling, that allows us to become more present—which leads to my next example.

"I am a present mommy."

When you have a conversation with your kiddo, how often does your brain wander to a work project? Or how often are you at your kid's soccer game, but you miss their goal because you were too busy scanning through work emails? Instead of beating yourself up right now thinking of all the times you weren't present, I want you to set an affirmation that next time, you will be.

This one is simple. You know when you need to be present. Make the affirmation and do it.

"I am a caring daughter."

Every few months, my mom comes to visit me, see her grandkids, and just have some time around family. Without fail, when she arrives I usually have one hundred things I need to do. I bustle in from my workday, meet everyone in the kitchen, start making dinner, and need to parent my kids, who decide to act extra bananas whenever we have company.

I decide to go bananas as well. When my parents visit me, I get extra conscious and aware of all the things that go wrong—and then I worry about not showing up "perfect." While I know it is all silly and that my mom and dad will love me no matter what, I tend to get a little edgy when either of them comes to visit. Because I know I am being prickly and I don't know why, I find myself exhausted and just wanting to retreat to bed. It is sometimes easier to be nothing. But that is not fair to me or to my mom or my dad.

While there are times I legitimately cannot keep my eyes open after 8:15 when my mom is here, there are other times when I know I need to try harder and make a real effort to simply just "be" a daughter. While there are times I really do not want to alter my morning routine when my dad is here, I also know that our quiet conversations over morning coffee are ones we cherish and are always worth it.

Wouldn't you know that every time I write in my journal, "I am a caring daughter," "I am an attentive daughter," "I am a listening daughter," those are my favorite evenings with my mom? If I write the same the day before a visit with my dad, even if I don't get the time to journal on the morning he is here, it sticks with me and allows me to slow down and break away from my routine in the morning so I am spending some quality time with him?

Somehow, my patience with the kids increases, I am not as snappy, and I make the time to truly listen, sit on the couch, pour a glass of wine without worrying how I will feel in the morning, and be present. I make time to break away from my book or computer and sit and relax at the kitchen table with my dad.

Now that you have an idea of how affirmations can set you up for the day you want by creating *who* you will show up as that day and the actions you will take, what affirmations do you know will be useful to you? Who do you need to show up as today? Tomorrow? This weekend? Next Wednesday? What do you have going on during those days? What matters the most? Who do you need to *be* so that everything else will go smoothly?

Journaling—Gratitude

Research study upon research study has shown that when you express gratitude, your happiness will increase.

I have two "tricks" to practicing gratitude to make it sink in deeper and truly drop down into your heart.

First, the more specific the gratitude, the better. Instead of just writing down "I am grateful for my kids," I like to write "I am so grateful for this family that I yearned and longed for when I was back in seventh grade and just wanted an intact family with a brother and a sister and a dog." Instead of just "my coffee," I like to write, "My Nespresso machine that makes me a double espresso every morning with no mess and helps me wake up and gets things moving."

Second, when you are scanning your brain and heart for gratitude, I want you to see it in "movie" form. Then watch the internal movie and attempt to feel the moment that you are grateful for. Let it really solidify into a "core" memory, like the ones from the movie *Inside Out*. Watch the "movie" until you feel a smile tugging at the corners of your mouth.

If you take just a tiny bit of time to think about what you are grateful for each morning, a really neat thing starts to happen. As you go through each day, you start to look for things to be grateful for to capture the next morning. Once you start noticing them, you start to feel each moment of gratitude more fully and in real time. Your thoughts will begin to pick up on this and will tell you, *I am in a moment of gratitude right now! Slow down! Cherish this. Look around. Take a moment.* When this happens, truly feel it in your bones and in your smile. Then say, "I don't have to wait until the morning to feel gratitude. I can feel it now! I can feel it in the experience!"

That right there, my friend? That is mindfulness. Yes, it can be that simple. Pay attention to the world around you, find gratitude in the moments big and small, and let yourself feel it while you are in it.

Journaling—Concrete Way I Will Plug into My Family

Are you beginning to understand why journaling can be incredibly effective? How it can change the trajectory of your day? How it can improve your overall outlook on life and thus your happiness? Here is another of my favorite prompts: What is a concrete way I will "plug in" to my family today?

Sometimes, days go by where you are so caught up in the routine that, when you go to bed, you might wonder, *Did I actually converse with my kid or spouse today beyond "How was school?" "What do you*

97

want in your lunch?" or "Put on your socks!"? Did I actually LOOK at my children today, or was I so caught up in the routine of getting out the door, working, getting kids back from school, supervising homework, making dinner, dealing with sibling squabbles, overseeing the bedtime routine, and falling asleep myself that I forgot to actually LOOK at them? Even more so, did I actually SEE them? Did I look into their eyes and behind their expressions and see if anything was underneath? Did I attempt to connect with them beyond telling them what to do and making sure all of their boxes were checked for the day? Did I make myself available if they wanted to talk to me?

I know—we are already doing all of the things. The good news? This task is simple in terms of an idea and execution. You just need to pick one thing, one way that you know you are showing up 100% in that moment in time.

It could be a really good hug with your kid at the end of the day, where you don't let go right away and you bite your tongue with all the reminders that you want to give them. Instead, you are just in that hug.

It could be putting down your phone at the soccer game.

It could be a nature discovery walk with your daughter while you're at your son's baseball practice.

It could be saying yes to making them lunch, even though they usually do it themselves.

It could be a dance party in the kitchen.

It could be blasting their favorite music on the drive to school, even though you hate that song.

It could be actually getting in the pool and playing "Colors."

It could be reading a chapter of your son's favorite book to him.

It could be playing hide-and-seek.

It could be taking the time to "research" one of their favorite YouTubers with them.

It could be an "impromptu" pillow fight (totally planned by you, but a big fun surprise for the kids).

It could be making sure you are home from work in time to have a sit-down dinner at the kitchen table with the whole family.

The trick here is that it doesn't have to be some big, grandiose, long drawn-out thing. It does not have to be a three-hour arts and crafts or LEGO marathon. The truth is, the kids usually have their own things they want to do, and they don't demand hours upon hours from us as they get older. Yet they do relish the check-in and when we go off our normal course to spend meaningful time with them. Even though they don't always show it or express it, they do pick up on it. They just need to see you 100% engaged in one small way. The trick is to think about it before you are there—and to be 100% there.

GRIT-WORK

If you decide that you want to try out journaling as your anchor, head on over to your **GRIT-workbook** and start today! In your **GRIT-workbook**, I give you worksheets to track your affirmations, gratitude, and concrete ways you can plug into your family. Feel free to make as many copies as you like. Also, as I shared with you in a footnote a few pages ago, check out the sparkle & GRIT journal!

Anchor 4: MEDITATION

I fought this anchor for such a long time, even though I was aware of the benefits of meditation. You know, practicing meditation *only* reduces stress, gives you a sense of peace and calm, manages symptoms of anxiety, asthma, cancer, and insomnia[12] . . . like, why start something

---

12. Mayo Clinic Staff, "Meditation: A Simple, Fast Way to Reduce Stress," Mayo Clinic, April 29, 2022, https://www.mayoclinic.org/tests-procedures/meditation/in-depth/meditation/art-20045858.

that can do all those things? Why spend some time sitting in blissful peace and quiet? (Ha, I know.) The thought of just sitting there felt like a wave of anxiety on its own. So, just like I used to skip the Savasana pose in yoga for an embarrassingly long time, I also skipped out on giving myself time to meditate.

Then I heard a Zen proverb that goes something like this: "Meditate for twenty minutes every day. If you are too busy for that, meditate for an hour." I felt particularly called out and I said, "Okay Wendy, it is time to add *something*." I started dabbling in short five-minute meditations I found on the Peloton app, only doing them sporadically, and with no real rhyme or reason. While I liked them (and still do), I didn't experience the pure, beautiful, blissful power of meditation until I attended a spiritual retreat in February 2023. One word: wow. It is hard to explain what those longer sessions do for you. While in them, you feel like you are transcending space and time. I have experienced pure bliss, healing, giddiness, and true peace. After I came home from the February retreat, I started searching for longer guided meditations (sometimes an hour long!) and now I do those on Sunday afternoons when I can escape the rest of my family. On the days when I don't have a full hour, I add in a quick five-minute session. I have come to find there is no wrong way to meditate—it just matters that you set aside the time and do it.

While I am still in the "baby stages" of creating my meditation practice, I have found one thing to be for sure: every time I spend even just five minutes in meditation, I feel an unparalleled sense of peace and grounding.

My advice to you if you are ready to take on meditation as your anchor: Go in slow. Opt to begin your weekday mornings with a five- to ten-minute meditation on a subject that resonates with you. (For example, on the Peloton app, you can choose Kindness, Calming,

Energizing, Happiness, etc.) Once a week, head over to YouTube and find a longer guided meditation and gift yourself the time to just be in it. I recommend guided meditations because I find I can better quiet my mind and really sink into a longer meditation when I am given a visual of what I "should" be seeing and experiencing behind closed eyes. Looking for extra credit? Search your local community and see if anyone is hosting an in-person meditation. There is something powerful about doing meditations in person and with a practiced guide.

The Chain Reaction Effect of Anchors

The neat thing about anchors is that when you decide on and commit to one of them, it doesn't mean you are stuck with "just" that one. When I decided to "sweat" every day, it began a beautiful chain reaction of events, allowing me to build anchor on top of anchor—all of the ones I just told you about and then some.

Sweat

Sweat began all of this. I had a program to plug into every day, and I was laser-focused on "just" getting in those twenty-five minutes. When I woke up in the morning, my only focus was on getting downstairs and pushing Play.

Sweat → Passion and "Waking Up"

Sweat led me to discover a new group of online friends who encouraged me to try entrepreneurship in the form of health and wellness coaching. I fell in love. Remember that 1997 High School Cross-Country Captain Wendy? The bubbly one walking down the hallway, smiling at everyone she saw? The one who was known to pour encouragement into others? She was *back*. I felt like I could finally breathe again. The funny thing? Until I started breathing again, I never realized I was holding my breath.

Before I knew it, I was setting the alarm clock even earlier than 6 a.m. so I could begin my days coaching these women. This kind of "work" was so different from my job as a lawyer, and I loved it so much that literally, no joke, I was bounding out of bed in the morning. I was excited when my alarm went off because I *got to* do this work. A fire was lit.

I was on the precipice of realizing that sweat was going to change the trajectory of my life. Being thrust into a new group of women who had some of the most amazing business minds made me think, *Hmm. If she was able to leave her corporate job and start something totally different and new, why can't I?* But then I got scared and itchy and discontent. My fear turned into me being snappy at home and retreating at work. I didn't fit in anymore anywhere. Which leads me to the next layer.

Sweat → Passion and "Waking Up" → Reading

It was in my new business venture that I learned about reading personal development. When I was down in the dumps, my business and wellness coach at the time, Chrisanthi, would always say, "Well, what are you reading for personal development?" I typically blew her off—until one day I didn't. I had mastered waking up before the kids, I had mastered working out pretty much every day, I was having fun in this new online business world, and yet I was still feeling a little "off." Stepping outside of my comfort zone as I started this online venture brought new challenges. A whole new set of self-limiting beliefs. A whole new set of goals and dreams. I did not see how any of it was going to actually happen for me, and it had me very much up in my head.

I finally said, "Okay, what should I read first?" I took her suggestion and began Mel Robbins's *The Five Second Rule*.

Looking at my Audible history, I purchased this first "personal development" book in September 2017. As I am sitting here writing *this* book, that timeline is making my jaw drop. I made the leap of faith to leave my firm in June 2018, opened my doors in August 2018, and then became a certified life coach in August 2021. That is how fast these books woke up something inside of me and lit a fire under my ass.

Sweat → Passion and "Waking Up" → Reading
→ Connection and Community

My sweat led me to find a group of friends who have become my ride or die. We started off as simply online workout buddies. Now? They are my rock. They call me out on my shit. Everything is on the table with them, and nothing is left off. We each fiercely want the others to succeed in all areas of their lives. And it all started with sweat.

In your adult life, do you ever have the feeling that you no longer have friends who "get you"? Or worse, do you feel like you have friends who really don't seem to like it when you succeed or when you are happy? Your group might be out there waiting for you. Finding your anchor could very well lead you to them.

Sweat → Passion and "Waking Up" → Reading
→ Connection and Community → Writing/Journaling

My sweat led me to pursue what I really wanted out of life and inspired me to develop the new skills I would need to succeed as a coach. Part of my discovery process was starting a blog and falling in love with writing again. Not only was I writing fun social media posts and blog articles to help connect with women like you, but I also started writing for myself every day in the form of journaling. Every day, I started the day asking, "Who do I want to be today?"

Writing, for me, is so much more than putting words on paper. It is a transcendent experience. It teleports me back to my past. It is cathartic, therapeutic, enlightening, crushing, eye-opening, and joyous, all in one. It connects me to my past and future selves. Best of all? It connects me with you, my readers. If I can write just one sentence to help get you through the day, disrupt a negative thinking pattern, help you feel heard and validated, or perhaps even transform your life, then I know I have made a difference, and I can breathe and smile deeper.

If writing can do this for me, what can it do for you?

Sweat → Passion and "Waking Up" → Reading
→ Connection and Community → Writing/Journaling → Meditation

As you may be gathering, sweat was just the beginning. Sweat eventually brought me to a meditation practice that has healed wounds I have carried since I was a small child. Not only that, but on the days I engage in meditation, I am just an overall better human. End stop. Period.

Sweat → Waking Up before the Kids → Passion and "Waking Up"
→ Reading → Connection and Community → Writing/Journaling
→ Here, Right the Heck Now

Sweat led to waking up before the kids, which led me to my passion, which led me to the most amazing mentors in the world, which led me to my best of friends and advisers and coaches, which led me to writing and led me to you. Once I saw that friends, colleagues, and professionals at large were curious about and inspired by what I had to say, I dug in deep and amplified. When I heard from various friends and acquaintances *and even judges* that they began to make some real changes in their lives because of posts I wrote or stories I shared, I knew I was onto something. All of those steps and wins and morning routine components led me to become an author and a coach.

Do you see how it is all connected?

Sweat, for me, has been the anchor, the glue, the double espresso that keeps me going. The beginning to all of this. Sweat was the first seed sown that led to all things sparkle & GRIT.

What does that mean for you? It is time for you to find your anchor. Then, when that one anchor is set in place, you will have the capacity to add the next one, and then the next. Incredible transformation and a technicolor life are just an anchor away. If I had a dollar for every time I have seen, heard, or witnessed this layering of anchors phenomenon firsthand (especially those beginning with sweat), I would be a rich woman!

Now it's your turn! What is it going to be? What are you willing to try? Do you see how a morning routine is *so much more* than "just" a morning routine?

Unless and until you dip a toe into the morning routine water, you won't know what opportunities might open for you. I know that can be exhilarating and scary all at once. I get it. I get that it is scary to peek behind the door of possibilities you may have closed off long ago. But can you take the risk of what might happen if you don't at least try?

· Every time I think about it—what if I didn't start that T25 workout back in 2015? What if I blew off waking up early? What if I didn't join that accountability group? What if I didn't say yes to entrepreneurship? What if I didn't say yes to my coach pushing me to read personal development? What if I didn't start a blog? What if I didn't hire Nakia, my first coach, to push me 1:1? What if I didn't follow my heart and make the big, scary, life-altering decisions? Where would I be?—I am grateful that I do not have to know.

Setting the Finish Line the Night Before

There is a super important nugget in here to ensure your morning routine actually works: you need to start it the night before.

What, Wendy? That doesn't make sense!

Au contraire my friend. As you will see, it is everything. And it is more than just laying out your workout clothes and shoes for the next day, although that is a *great* practice. Instead, we are going to sprinkle in some more mindfulness, this time in the evening.

At night, after your kids are going to bed, are your usual debates, "Should I hop on the computer and bang out some more emails?" "What series should I start on Netflix?" "Cabernet or Old Fashioned?" "SkinnyPop or break out the Girl Scout cookies hidden somewhere in the freezer?"

If you find yourself asking these questions, usually beginning around 4 p.m. as you finally see the end of your workday in sight and then again around 8 p.m. as bedtime is looming, I want you to pause for a minute and ask yourself *the* most important question. The million-dollar question. If you can remember to ask yourself this question and follow through, this is the one question that will give tomorrow's you the best chance of feeling like a rock star.

"Who do I want to show up as tomorrow morning?"

Then ask these follow-up questions to help flesh it out:

"How do I want to feel?"

"Am I okay with feeling foggy and headache-y?"

"Do I want to feel groggy all day tomorrow?"

"What important things do I have going on tomorrow, and how can I best show up to them? What will hold me back?"

"What do I care about more, having this popcorn and staying up late or showing up on time to my OTF class and getting some major splat points?"

While writing this book, one particular set of questions came up for me time and time again: "What do I care about more on a Friday night? Letting loose and drinking wine and partying it up (by "party," I mean pajamas, the aforementioned popcorn, and hanging on the couch) or using my extended Saturday morning weekend time to get an hour or two of writing in with a clear head?"

Do you see that we need to make a choice at night to determine how our morning routine will go? Do you see how our morning routine actually begins the night before?

Let's see how sparkle & GRIT can help us here. sparkle is what drives you to have the best tomorrow you can. sparkle helps you envision your best self and allows you to get really excited and motivated about the bright shiny version of yourself that yearns to sweat, journal, and read. GRIT makes you do the damn thing, which here means lots (and lots) of conversations with yourself and then powering through. GRIT is taking the minute and making yourself look inward. Asking what will actually make you feel better. Not just living in what feels good in the here and now, but what feels good to tomorrow morning's version of you. GRIT is the mental stamina to look inward and not give up and give in.

When all else fails, what's your best bet if you are feeling worn and really struggling, and TV and cookies are calling your name? Go the eff to sleep.

After the nights you utilized your GRIT and listened to your sparkly self, do yourself a favor the next morning. When you wake up in the morning, before you get out of bed, do a body scan. How does your body feel? Wiggle your toes, move your legs, unscrunch your shoulders. Take note of where you are holding tension and where you feel relaxed. Are you feeling rested? Sore, but from-your-workout sore? Luxurious? As you scan to the top of your head, what do you notice? Clear head? Less foggy? How are you feeling emotionally? Peaceful? Clear? A sense of calm you have been missing?

Remember this feeling. It will serve you well.

GRIT-work

CRAFTING YOUR MORNING ROUTINE

I am so excited for this part! It is time for us to sit down together and craft *your* morning routine! Eek! If you aren't excited yet, don't worry. I have enough excitement for the both of us.

First, we are going to make this simple, and we are going to pay close attention to what is already, nonnegotiably, on your plate.

What time *must* you be out the door?

How long does it take you to get ready? Can you shorten any of that? Can you lay out your work clothes the day before? Have you fallen in love with dry shampoo? Are you dilly-dallying? Is there time in here that you don't need to be spending? If you take out the social media scrolling, how much time do you really need?

Now it's time to think about some tweaks when it comes to the kids.

What must *you* do each morning to help get the kids ready and out the door? Are your kids old enough to start packing their own lunches and filling up their own water bottles? If you are married or living with another adult, what can *they* do to help get the kids ready and out the door?

What can the kids do to help your household and take something off of your plate in the morning? (2023 was the year that our kids began unloading the dishwasher every morning. #lifechanging)

Remember, your morning routine starts the night before.

When is your bedtime? Can you make it earlier? Before you fight me, think about these questions: When you lie your head on your pillow, are you watching TV? Scrolling social media? Talking with your partner? Going straight to sleep? What can you tweak? How much joy are you really deriving from watching your millionth TikTok about a stupidly organized and extremely unrealistic fridge? Do you really need to see how the PTA president is setting her table for the holidays? Is it imperative that you know what a certain housewife had for dinner that day? No. What is imperative? *You.* Your health. *Your* tomorrow morning.

Let's lay it out so you can see it. I also include this timeline in your **GRIT-workbook** so you can play with it there as well.

Evening

Say no to   _____ p.m.

Turn off screens and social media   _____ p.m.

Go to bed   _____ p.m.

Morning

Wake up (no snooze)   _____ a.m.

Wander/stumble/prance into bathroom
and put on workout clothes   _____ a.m.

Drink 12 oz of water (and caffeine
/adaptogenic drink of choice)   _____ a.m.

PICK ONE

Sweat   _____ a.m.

Read   _____ a.m.

Journal   _____ a.m.

Meditate   _____ a.m.

Get ready

Self   _____ a.m.

Get kids up/help get kids ready   _____ a.m.

Ten-Minute Buffer

Leave house/kids on bus/start day!   _____ a.m.

Things to remember:

1) If all you can manage is waking up before the kids and drinking coffee alone for the time being—that is okay!
2) This will take some trial and error—and that is okay!
3) Some days, this will all go to shit—and that is okay!
4) If you decide that your workout time makes more sense after work (and you have proven to yourself that working out in the evening is something you can and will consistently do)—that is okay!
5) If you figure out that you only blow out your hair two days a week and that eats up all of your morning time, but that the other days you then have plenty of time for all the things—that is okay!
6) The key? You keep coming back. You are consistent. You figure out your anchor. As you know, my anchor was—and still is—sweat. Even when I have a super early flight and only have a tiny bit of time, I still make my way down to the basement and take ten minutes to move my body in some sort of way. I don't know how not to anymore.
7) Pay attention during this trial-and-error time. What works? What does not? Keep adjusting until you have found the right morning routine for you.
8) Don't be surprised if you find you love your routine so much that you stick to it on the weekends too.
9) Once you have mastered sweat, read, or journal, add in the next one. Once you have mastered two of them, add in a third. Go back to the beginning of this chapter, when you ranked your GRITTY morning routine activities. Which ones got a low score? Which ones can you start to add in?

I would love to hear what you chose as your anchor and how it is working out for you. If you are someone who shares their morning routine on social media, I would be honored if you added the hashtags #sparkleandGRIT and #sparkleandGRITmorning routine to your posts. I would love this opportunity to cheer you along!

CHAPTER 6
Predicting the Future

"A Million Dreams," *The Greatest Showman*

In chapter 5, we talked about setting an affirmation for the day via journaling. You saw how writing one simple line in the morning can change the trajectory of your whole day. This piece is so important that we need to dig in even deeper. This is the secret sauce to the whole enchilada. You are the number one person who gets to decide your future. Giving yourself the best future possible is why you are reading this, right?

In this chapter, you will understand that you can change your brain so that it works *for* you rather than *against* you. You will learn that you can fool your brain into believing that the best things have already happened to you, priming you to experience them again (and again). *You* are your best (and only) bet to living the life you desire.

Future-Casting Overview

What is future-casting, exactly? (You know, I actually thought I invented the term on my own until I heard others start to use it as well!) Googling it, you will find all sorts of meanings, but here is my definition.

Future-casting is closing your eyes and playing a movie inside of your head with regard to a particular situation before it happens. When you future-cast, you visualize yourself as a third-party onlooker (akin to an out-of-body experience) or you play out a scenario as yourself (like a dream where you are awake and in control). While in this visualization, you are aware of how you talk, how you move, how you conduct yourself, what your surroundings smell like and even taste like, how the wind flows through your hair, how the air is circulating around your body, everything. During the mind movie, you are checking in with how you feel as you move through the experience. The more particular you get, the better. You can choose your clothes, how you will respond to those around you, your level of confidence, and how you carry yourself.

Future-casting is a way of planning ahead and playing out different scenarios until you land on the one that clicks for you. You literally get to walk around in the future.

The beauty?

Once that same scenario presents itself in real life, you are prepared. Just as an actor has a dress rehearsal before a play, you get to have a dress rehearsal for any event you know you have coming up. You get to decide how you will talk, how you will answer, how you will conduct yourself, and even how you will feel.

How wild is that?

Curious how this works? I am about to take you on a very brief (and basic!) neuroscience lesson.

You have the ability to change your brain!

What?!

Crazy, right?

The term is "neuroplasticity," defined as "the brain's ability to change and adapt due to experience."[13] I also like this way of describing it. Neuroplasticity . . .

refers to the physiological changes in the brain that happen as the result of our interactions with our environment. From the time the brain begins to develop in utero until the day we die, the connections among the cells in our brains reorganize in response to our changing needs. This dynamic process allows us to learn from and adapt to different experiences.[14]

For example, think of a time where you burned yourself on a hot stove. Your brain now knows to move your hand away when there is a potential of getting burned. The next time you are close to a hot surface, you remove your hand quickly, you don't mess around, and the damage is minimal.

Sadly, the connections made in our brain don't always help us. In fact, sometimes they hinder us, scare us, or keep us in bad habits. For example, maybe there was a time you spoke in public in the third grade, and you tripped on stage and fell flat on your face, your skirt flew up, and everyone saw your polka-dotted underwear and laughed and laughed. You were called Polka-Dot Nancy for years. Now, when you are presented with a public-speaking opportunity, you are immediately overcome with fear and anxiety and feel your blood start to bubble. Instead of ever saying yes to an opportunity that would

13. Kendra Cherry, "What Is Neuroplasticity?" Verywell Mind, updated November 8, 2022, https://www.verywellmind.com/what-is-brain-plasticity-2794886.

14. Courtney E. Ackerman, "What Is Neuroplasticity? A Psychologist Explains [+14 Tools]," Positive Psychology, July 25, 2018, https://positivepsychology.com/neuroplasticity/.

further your career, your brain connects public speaking to fear to danger and humiliation and, before you know it, you squeak out a "no thank you" and extricate yourself from the awkward conversation as fast as humanly possible.

Now here's the good news.

Once we understand that we can *choose* to forge new connections in our brains, connections that inspire us and propel us forward, we can reverse engineer the system and make our brains work for us!

For example, have you ever broken the habit of soda, cigarettes, or candy? Do you remember the time when you could never imagine *not* cracking open a Coke for lunch, lighting up a cigarette on the drive to work, or eating candy at 3 p.m.? Yet, at some point, after giving it up, replacing the behavior, or just plain old breaking the habit, your urge to reach for a Coke, find your lighter, or head to the vending machine started to go away. After a while, it was just a whisper. Congrats! Somewhere along the way, you set up a detour in the road map of your brain, creating a new connection and cancelling out the old one.

That was your crash course in neuroplasticity. I find that when I understand the *why* behind something, it makes it that much easier to try something new.

Now that we know that we can change our brains and how they fire, this leads us to the next cool thing about how our minds work. Our brains, from a neuroscience perspective, have a hard time telling the difference between what we actually experience in real physical life and our imagination of what we experience through visualization.[15] This means that, when we visualize getting out of a thought spiral, saying no to a treat, running a race, or confidently delivering a speech,

---

15. University of Colorado at Boulder, "Your Brain on Imagination: It's a Lot Like Reality, Study Shows," ScienceDaily, December 10, 2018, https://www.sciencedaily.com/releases/2018/12/181210144943.htm.

our brains believe we already did it! What does that mean when we pair it with what we learned from the mini lesson on neuroplasticity? That with our thoughts alone, we can carve new pathways. With our thoughts alone, we can fool our brains into things we want to experience as if we have already experienced them.

I realize I have barely broken the surface here on all the neat things involving neuroscience, but here is your takeaway: You have the ability to change your brain. You have the ability to disrupt the nonsense. When you visualize the future and the life you want to live, day in and day out, not only do you help disrupt the patterns you are trying to break away from, but you are also priming your brain to keep taking the path you want because your brain thinks you have already done it! How cool is that?

What does this mean for you? If you give yourself the time to spend on visualization, you will become the version of "you" you want to be faster and with less resistance. Let's get to it already.

Future-Casting Your Marriage

There's a John Gottman quote that has always stuck with me:

> *Trust is built in very small moments, which I call 'sliding door' moments . . . In any interaction, there is a possibility of connecting with your partner or turning away from your partner.*
>
> *. . . One such moment is not important, but if you're always choosing to turn away, then trust erodes in a relationship— very gradually, very slowly.*[16]

16. John Gottman, "John Gottman on Trust and Betrayal," *Greater Good Magazine*, October 29, 2011, https://greatergood.berkeley.edu/article/item/john_gottman_on_trust_and_betrayal.

The first time I heard that quote, I felt like I got slapped in the face. Wasn't I doing exactly that? Turning away? At every moment? Were all of my small, seemingly innocuous actions leading to something awful?

Remember how I hid from my husband in the kitchen? Or the time I could barely tear myself away from the computer to say goodbye? Where else was I unknowingly eroding our marriage?

Didn't I know better as a family law attorney? Hadn't I heard horror story after horror story? How many times had husbands confessed to me that they didn't even think their wives liked them anymore? Wasn't I showing the same thing to mine? How often did I ask clients, "When did you last go out on a date—just the two of you—no other couples?" and get blank stares, furled lips, or sighs? How often in mediation did I see couples sitting across from me with their arms hugged tightly into themselves, angry, physically turning their whole bodies so they didn't even have to look at each other?

What the freak was I doing? This was exactly the trajectory I had told myself I would never take. As I shared with you earlier, my parents divorced when I was about nine years old. What kept me up at night as a kid? What did I wish and yearn for through all of my middle school and high school years? I would have given anything to have an intact family—a mom, dad, sibling, and me (and a Siberian husky named Chucks). I wanted togetherness and that sense of truly belonging. I could not wait until I was an adult and could start my own family unit.

Why was I turning away? I had the family I had wished and prayed so hard for. My kids had exactly what I had wanted for myself all those years. But more than that, I had a husband who was everything I wanted him to be and everything he needed to be. Why couldn't I just give him common courtesy and a flipping chance? He cared about me, he loved me, he wanted to take care of me, he loved taking care of the kids. I had everything in my arsenal to create the life and family I always wanted; why was I giving it up for wine, snacks, and *The Good Wife*?

I made the decision to turn in.

Weirdly, this wasn't easy at first. I was so used to being annoyed, huffy, eye-rolling, and self-centered that it took work. While all the "greats" said marriage is hard work, I didn't think this was what they meant, that it took work to actively *be* in the marriage. To actively care. To actively love. Even when I was so damn tired and wrung out I didn't feel like it.

What did I do?

I used that handy-dandy neuroscience tool. First, I needed to see the paths that I had paved. I put on my investigator hat and put myself on hyperalert to see where I was "turning away." I boldly shone a light on where I wasn't showing up as the wife I wanted to be. I spent time visualizing how I would react in different situations and focusing on all of the places I would start to turn in instead of turning away.

For starters, I discovered that when my husband went to kiss me, I pulled away or got annoyed that he was in my space. I began to turn in. (I know, I sound like a total monster. But I am guessing I am not the only one here who started this practice accidentally and then it turned into weeks/months/years of actively turning away.)

At night, when I *just* wanted to zone out but he wanted to actually have a conversation, I saw that I got very huffy and puffy. I began to turn in.

When he had an idea, I shut it down, assuming mine was better. I began to turn in and listen (and realized he had some amazing ideas too, sometimes way better than mine).

I discovered that, instead of telling him about my struggles or successes, I would just tell my girlfriends and then not feel like rehashing them all over again. I began to turn in and call him first.

See the theme here?

Do any of these resonate with you?

I also began to evaluate my friendships. What friendships thrived on conversations where we put down our husbands? The constant complaining? The stories of mutual misery? Those conversations weren't serving me, my marriage, or, quite frankly, my friends' marriages either. If I couldn't turn a conversation around, I got off the phone. I lost friends in this process, but I gained a better partnership with my husband.

I also paid attention to who we were spending the most time with. We used to be friends with another couple. As much as I loved her, and as much as my husband loved him, *every* time we hung out with them, it brought out the worst in us. If they yelled, we yelled. If they bickered, we bickered. It almost felt like a competition for whose husband was driving them more batty. When we returned home from hanging with them for the evening, the fighting didn't end. It was like we were hungover and addicted to this behavior. The griping, bitching, and eye-rolling would stick around for at least another few days until it finally got out of our systems. We don't hang out with them anymore.

Future-casting the marriage you want is more than just getting rid of the bad stuff and turning in. It is also figuring out *who* you want to be in a marriage. Is there anyone you want to emulate? Is there anyone in your life who you hang out with who makes you want to be a better partner?

During my period of turning in, I was lucky enough to have a long weekend with my friends Elizabeth and Stef (yes, the same Elizabeth and Stef from chapter 3 with the lottery comment!). To give you some backstory, this was *the* absolutely hardest month of our marriage. This was the month where everything went to shit. All of a sudden, the cumulative effect of all of our disagreements, fighting, nagging, and both of us actively turning away came to a head.

That weekend was life-changing (I don't even know if Elizabeth and Stef know this!). Besides eating our way through Brooklyn all weekend and watching the most amazing intimate performance by Megan Hilty in a tiny theater of like one hundred people, I could not get over how *nice* Elizabeth and Stef were to one another. Like, truly nice. Truly caring. Truly wanting to make sure the other was happy and content. Even if and when they disagreed about something, they approached it so gently. "Hey babe, I know . . . , but can we . . . instead?" in the kindest tone. No snark. No eye rolls. It was like I was watching the most pure form of love go back and forth between these two. I was in awe. In every moment, they turned in.

I pledged I would be more like them once I got home.

Of course, it didn't work quite like that. I went from a love bubble to a real-life bubble. While I had gotten to experience all of their wonderfulness, my hubs had not. He was used to the old way of doing things and used to the old me. Our crappy tone with one another took over.

My love bubble burst.

But I was ready to turn in.

It was time to actively show up and decide what kind of wife I wanted to be. Remember that story I told you about the amazing hug I shared with my husband, due to my "I am a loving wife" affirmation? My time with Eliz and Stef got me to that moment. That is the epitome of the marriage I want. That is what we both work hard for now. That is the product of turning in and to one another over and over.

That moment taught me the secret sauce for how to show up as the best wife, which would give me the best chance and the best marriage. I had to plan for it. I had to see it and visualize it before it happened.

I had to look for the moments where I could "turn in" and "turn to," as John Gottman puts it. This is what I call "future-casting" when it comes to marriage. It didn't happen overnight. It didn't happen without me planning for it. It happened with intention, reminders, work, and turning in, even when I was not in the mood to.

I think sometimes we overcomplicate how we can be great spouses. I think a lot of the time it is easier to find fault with all the things your partner is doing to drive you batty. Instead, how can you future-cast yourself and decide who you want to be?

Future-Casting at Work

We also get to decide who we want to be at work every day. We get to decide how we will respond to an asinine opposing counsel (or boss or coworker). We have a choice on whether or not we will let these types of people get under our skin and how we will react in the moment.

Let me tell you about "Skip." Skip was counsel for a parent in a grueling custody case I had several years ago. He was awful. More than awful. Merely because my position on the matter didn't match his, he took every word I said and turned it against me in a tone that was so obviously condescending, it was almost comical. When we finally met at the courthouse, shortly after I had found out that he had brought my kid clients to open court without my permission (and then compounded the matter by trying to sneak my kid clients into the judge's chambers), I lost my shit. Before I could have a rational thought, I approached him, angry, shaking, and talking very fast, and told him to never, *ever*, bring my clients to court again without my approval.[17]

---

17. For those of you who are not attorneys, or perhaps not familiar with child counsel work, what Skip had done was a big no-no. Huge.

Calmly, slowly, and with intention, this man turned to me and said, "Why, Ms. Meadows. You seem angry."

The way he said "Ms. Meadows" and his apparent complete lack of concern that he was being totally unethical made me *seethe*. I lost it even more. *"You bet I am angry!"*

I stormed off to find a place to cool down before more words could come out of my mouth. My brain was going a million miles a minute and I could not form a coherent sentence. I felt emotionally beat-up and unprepared.

A few months later, I was on the phone with Skip, trying to help the mom and dad figure out visitation for the weekend. Skip, as always, accused me of all sorts of nonsense and bias, taking any opportunity he could to throw me under the bus. When I tried to stand up for myself and said something like, "Look, Skip, I am sick and tired of this. Please *stop*. I know what you are doing, and it is getting old. Stop implying that I am acting unethical in some way," his response? "I am really endearing myself to you, aren't I, Ms. Meadows?" Ew and ugh.

And then—I had one of those cartoon mind bubbles pop out of my brain, saying loud and clear, "Wendy, he is doing all of this *on purpose!*" While one part of my brain said, "Fuck you" and "Never call me Ms. Meadows—or anything else—ever again, you condescending fuck," the other part said, "Ah-*ha*, he likes this shit. He actually likes this shit! His goal is to exasperate the hell out of me until I break and freak out. This is his freakin' plan. This is all a game to him!"

No more, Skip. Not playing.

I had three more court hearings with this man. Do you know what I did every single morning? First, I reminded myself of who I did not want to be. Then I took a deep breath and decided who I did want to be:

Calm. Cool. Collected.

Did he try to bait me? Of course he did. How did I respond? Cool indifference. I realized I could still do my job (an even better one, in fact), if I put up an invisible force field around me, blocking all of his insulting prose, not breaking a smile or a frown, raising an eyebrow, or changing my tone of voice. I just had to "be." By the third hearing, he stopped trying.

In addition to me being proud of myself for showing up as a stronger and more powerful woman, I also was able to increase my focus on the job at hand: representing my kid clients. Instead of wasting all of my emotional energy dealing with a misogynistic, clueless dude, I funneled it all into doing the best work I could for the people that actually mattered, the kids.

Sadly, dealing with this gentleman was not the only time I have had to put up with this nonsense. Try out this one; I don't even know if I can write it into justice. Let's chat about "Gino."

Gino was worse because he dripped condescension in the same way as Skip, yet he was an excellent trial attorney. (I hate writing down the truth of that statement.) If I had to picture Gino as a kid, he would be that bully in fourth grade, the one who trips the girl and all the other kids see it happen, but then he turns around to the teacher and says in a dumb voice, "Whaddaya mean?! It wasn't me. I swear. She actually tripped me!" Before you know it, somehow the girl is the one in recess detention, even though she was the one with skinned knees, crying and lying disheveled on the ground.

Now imagine fourth-grade Gino all grown up and with forty-plus years of trial experience.

Gino had this habit of taking every objection I made and then lobbing it back at me, but as an exaggerated personal attack against either me or my client. Nonstop. He twisted the testimony of my client constantly, stating things that were untrue and then guffawing when corrected. Trial was like a theatrical show to him. Yet the only audience was the judge, our clients, and myself. There is no jury to sway in a child custody trial (unless you're in Texas!).

The "best" part? When Gino had my client on the witness stand, he kept positioning his whole entire six-foot-five, 250-pound body right smack dab between me and my client so I could not see her while she was testifying. Every time I moved my chair left, he moved left; if I moved right, he moved right, always in my line of sight. It got so ridiculous that I finally scooted my chair backward by about twenty feet so I could see the whole entire courtroom, no matter what. The judge, who 100% got what was going on, said, "Ms. Meadows, feel free to move around the courtroom as you need to." Thank goodness for her.

As you can imagine, just the sight of this man made me want to morph into an angry chihuahua–pit bull mix. (Note: I love pits—both my pups, I am sure, have pit in them—but I'm just trying to get the right image in your head.)

And yet. As I had learned from dealing with Skip, anger, annoyance, and frantic frustration would get me nowhere. Responding from pure emotion, without a plan, would just place me into some sick weird game that I never wanted to be a part of (seriously, do they teach this somewhere?).

As I went into my last hearing with this man, I brought my future-casting A-game. Not only did I journal about who I wanted to show up as that day, but I wrote it smack-dab on top of my trial notepad: "I am patient, unflappable, and calm."

And I was. Again, all of my mental energy was put to the task at hand, rather than spent dealing with the nonsense (and there was a lot of nonsense, including counsel *very purposefully* referring to me as "Ms. Meadow"—no *s*), and I was able to ignore Gino's obvious slights. My mental warm-up gave me the stamina to focus on the law, my questions, and my argument to the judge. I spoke slower and with more intention. I future-casted myself into the lawyer I needed to be that day.

I am sure you have similar stories about opposing coworkers, bosses, counsel, bosses, partners, and even colleagues. And while it is "fun?" to commiserate and know we aren't the only ones, our clients deserve for us to put our best foot forward. They deserve for us to future-cast our work meetings, trials, hearings, and even phone calls. They have earned the right for us to give our best mental energy to advocate for them and our positions and to leave behind the emotions that only serve to trigger us. While we aren't going to remain calm 100% of the time—because, heck, we are human—we owe it to them, their wallets, and ourselves to try.

No matter the nature of your job, I would bet money that you have had a similar situation at your work. Who drives you the most nuts? How can you best change your actions, outlook, and mindset so that the next time you are in this situation, you will be ready?

Future-Casting While Out and About

Do you have a place you love to go, but every single time, something blows up in your face? For me, it's Chipotle. It's the only place I really enjoy fast food, probably because none of it hurts my stomach—and who doesn't love their guac? ("Yes, for the love of God, I know guac is extra, but just lay it on, please.") Sadly, while the food is amazing, I have had a whole slew of not-so-great ordering encounters.

But my bad Chipotle luck actually didn't start there. No, it all started with a *Subway* experience. It was in the middle of the pandemic, and restaurants and stores were starting to open again. My family decided to venture out to Target that day, masked up and on the lookout for paper towels and toilet paper, searching for something to *do* because we had been trapped in our house for so long. We were on edge, still terrified of the virus, and sort of afraid of people. On our way home, we passed a Subway, and as per usual, all of a sudden, my kids were starving and had to have Subway and nothing else. *Sigh.* Well, we had already ventured into one store. What was one more? When I peered through the window, I saw that the line was only about three people deep. I figured we would be in and out within five minutes flat. (I knew how to eye up and calculate a Subway line from my days as a Certified Sandwich Artist—also strangely back around 1997—but I digress.) Do you know how long that line of three, each person only ordering one sandwich, lasted? *Twenty-five minutes!* I am not exaggerating an iota. Scout's honor. Just ask my kids.

As the line droned on and on and I watched the complete inefficiency of whatever the heck slow-as-molasses-ness was happening behind the counter, I started to twitch, grow agitated, and suffocate behind my mask. Finally, it was our turn! We ordered two kid's meals. It took about ten minutes to make those two four-inch subs. When it came time to pay, the cash register dude told me it was extra for cookies, even though the kid's meal comes with cookies. When I pointed this out, he told me I hadn't ordered kid's meals (I had). I think we went back and forth with the same sentences about five times. After a minute or two of this, I lost my ever-loving mind. (Don't worry, no yelling, just a mini freakout and a whole lot of flustered.) I finally said, "I don't care! Just ring me up. Charge me for the cookies. I don't care. I need to get *out of*

127

here right now!!" I paid, ran out of there, ripped off my mask, and then made eye contact with my two kids, who were looking up at me with inquisitive "what-the-heck-was-that?" stares.

From then on, "Mommy going Subway" became a family saying. Very quickly, my new name became "Chipotle Karen" when I had three very similar experiences at three (different) Chipotles over the course of the next six months. At first, I chalked it all up to "Chipotle needs some help in the training department," until I realized that I, Wendy, "Ms. Meadows," was the common denominator. It was me. I was the problem.

The next time I went to my favorite burrito bowl joint, I took a deep breath before I walked inside. I promised *not* to be a "Chipotle Karen." And—get this? I wasn't. I showed up as the Wendy who remembered what it was like to work in fast food. When I encountered cool indifference from the line worker, I smiled anyway. When I saw that there was a line because there was only one poor soul behind the counter, busting her ass and doing her best, rather than get annoyed by the wait, I turned to the person behind me and said, "Wow, look at her go. She is all alone and working so hard. Props to her!" I smiled again at the employee as she was finishing my order. I tried to be the person she needed. I told her she was doing a good job.

That is how you future-cast when you are out and about. I know it may seem small and insignificant, but it matters. Kindness goes far, and we need more of it.

GRIT-work

I know I am not alone in needing to future-cast my marriage, my work life, and how I carry myself when I am out and about. It is time to grab your **GRIT-workbook** and decide your future.

1) At home, what do I wish was different from how it is now? What can I do to show up as that wife, partner, or mom? This week? Next weekend? On date night?

2) At work, what situation gets me all worked up again and again? What big meeting do I have coming up that I am dreading? Who am I dreading seeing at that meeting? What can I do to show up as the best version of myself so I am proud when I leave? So all of my mental energy is focused on the task at hand?

3) Am I best representing the human race when I am out and about? Where do I turn into a total asshole? Where can I do better? Where can I swap out my piss-poor attitude? Who do I need to be when I go into these situations? How do I remind myself of this?

CHAPTER 7
Tackling Your Workday

"You Gotta Be," Des'ree

I know your deep dark secrets. You are more behind at work than you would like to admit. You have files and papers scattered everywhere. It has become so overwhelming, and the pile is so big, that you don't even know where to start. You feel like the hamster running on the wheel, never actually getting anywhere.

Whether or not you are in love with your job, here are some truths you need to be aware of:

1) That food on the table? Your job paid for that.
2) The purpose you feel when a project is done well? Your job allowed for the circumstance for that feeling to occur.
3) The fact you need to show up every day? Your job provides you with accountability, every day, without fail.
4) Those fun things you do that cost money? Your job pays for them.
5) The coaching you were able to invest in? Your job allowed *you* to be the number one investor in your reimagined life.

What do you owe your boss, your clients, and yourself? Your best work. Otherwise, you are cheating your boss, your clients, and yourself. What happens when you cheat yourself? You feel awful, inadequate, less than. You rob yourself of the chance to grow and succeed. You rob yourself of seeing what you are truly capable of. The world needs and deserves for you to show up fully. You matter. So much.

Now that we have that settled, let's get down to business and figure out what you need to do each day to show up as the best version of you.

Time Management

Time management is *the* number one thing I work on with my clients when it comes to work. I love this topic so much that I travel to law firms across the state, helping entire organizations hone this skill.

Let's take a peek at a success story and zone in on my client, Lo. Lo has one of the most discerning, smart, and witty brains I know. Unfortunately, before our work together, all of that goodness was locked up inside of her head, and instead of getting her work done on time, she was drowning. She shared with me that her method of getting things done was almost entirely composed of her boss yelling at her: step 1) he scolded her for something that was overdue, and step 2) she would go on a mad dash to get it done. While her end product would be good, it would also be really late.

By the time she got to me, what had started as a snowball was in full-blown avalanche mode. She was so behind that she couldn't even name the projects on her list. She didn't have a method to look in one place and see the (long) list of things she needed to get done. She had files, sticky notes, and lists everywhere: all over her kitchen table, scattered around her office, in her purse, *everywhere*. And it wasn't just her work that was suffering. Her health was going downhill. She was referring to herself in derogatory terms: "unorganized," "hopeless," "a mess." Worse, she started to believe those names. The more she believed them, the worse the problems got. If she was hopeless and a mess, why not eat the crap? If she was hopeless and a mess, why even try to get to work on time? If she was unorganized, why start since she was just going to fail anyhow? Unhappy begets unhappy. Feeling like a mess at work begets feeling like a mess at home. Feeling hopeless at your job begets feeling hopeless in life.

When we began our work together, she was a naysayer. Ninety-nine percent of her believed there was no way she could change her spots. That's okay. We just needed that 1% that had some hope. We got down to work, and I am happy to report that in just a few months' time, Lo and I were able to turn things around. No longer is she feeding that bullshit to herself. She has a system. She has a habit. She has a plan. She is the one calling her colleagues to task and ensuring that work gets done. Waiting until something is past due to work on it is no longer her M.O., and she has systems and habits in place to keep her on track.

Does she fall off the wagon every now and then? Of course—she is human! Just like you are going to fall off the wagon too. It happens. The trick is falling back on your systems (the very ones we talk about here) instead of falling *into* your spiral. As time goes on, you start to wear in those good-for-you brain connections we talked about in chapter 6, and it gets easier and easier to follow these habits and get out of the spiral.

Time Management Step 1: Top Three Tasks/Projects

As soon as you sit down at your desk, before you look at email, before you answer the phone, before you start to get into working mode, I want you to write down three tasks/projects you are going to get done today.

I don't want you to pick the easy ones. It is imperative that you pick the ones that are due the most immediately or are the most pressing. It is also critical that you pick at least one task that you really do not want to do (the one you are dreading), a concept I learned from the book *Eat That Frog* by Brian Tracy.[18]

Time Management Step 2: *You* Are the CEO of Your Day

Let me guess: on more days than not, your work email controls your day. You have a steady stream of incoming requests, ranging from urgent to administrative to silly to junk. Your emails also have some hidden bombs in them, probably sent from a dude like Skip or Gino from the last chapter, and once you have read them, your head wants to pop off. Instead of focusing on the projects you know need to be done, and completing them on time, it is just "easier" to respond to the emails as they come in and in the order received.

Now I know, I know: you are about to argue with me that unless you have a completely "read" email inbox, you will become so crippled with anxiety that you won't be able to function.

I know you don't want to hear this, but the belief that a "clean" email inbox matters above *everything* else is rarely true.

When you focus on email first, you have made the (un)conscious decision to let everybody else be the CEO of your day. How does that make sense? Aren't *you* in charge of your day? Don't *you* know how best to use your time to get everything done?

Are you really going to let men like Skip and Gino be in charge of your day? That new deodorant company? Your daughter's third-grade

---

18. Brian Tracy, Eat That Frog!: 21 Great Ways to Stop Procrastinating and Get More Done in Less Time, Third Edition (Oakland, CA: Berrett-Koehler Publishers, 2017).

teacher? Rothy's marketing department? Do you hear me? Do you get what I am pointing out here?

But wait, there's more! It is not all your fault.

Did you know that every time we open an email, we are looking for a hit of dopamine? For those who don't remember what we learned in high school biology class, dopamine is commonly thought of as a "feel good" hormone. It is naturally released when we get enough sleep and exercise, smile, spend time in the sun, and listen to music.[19] Drugs such as opioids, cocaine, and nicotine also cause a surge of dopamine, leading to addiction.[20] In short, this hormone helps us link experiences with pleasure and makes us want to do those experiences again (and again). I first learned about the email dopamine hit/addiction when I listened to the Audible version of Mel Robbins's *The 5 Second Rule*, and now it is one of those things I cannot not know anymore. Mel likens our opening for unread emails to pulling the lever of a slot machine in Vegas. Just like the slot machine player expects a win behind each pull, we expect a "winning" email behind each scroll and open. Checking emails triggers the same release of dopamine as playing the slot machine. They are equally addictive. I am going to go out on a limb and say the email addiction is more chronic because email is accessible at every flipping moment.

How does it feel to know that email is like a drug? How does it feel to realize that we are letting men like Skip and Gino be our drug dealers? Pretty gross, huh? Do I have your attention yet?

---

19. Erica Julson, "10 Best Ways to Increase Dopamine Levels Naturally," Healthline, updated July 10, 2023, https://www.healthline.com/nutrition/how-to-increase-dopamine.

20. "How an Addicted Brain Works," Yale Medicine, May 25, 2022, https://www.yalemedicine.org/news/how-an-addicted-brain-works.

Here is the trick to Step 1 (writing down your three tasks/projects) and Step 2 (remembering that you are the CEO of your day). It is imperative that, until you become a masterful ninja and are able to glance at your email and not be tempted to clear it out and read emails that we both know can wait, you will need to ignore your email for a small portion of your day. Even better, do not check it until you are done with tasks/projects 1 and 2. Or give yourself set times and hours that you will devote to email. I have a client who checks it at 10, 1, and 4. Since moving to this new method, she is less distracted and more on top of her work than ever before.

What new habit can you adopt?

Time Management Step 3: Dings and Notifications

But, Wendy, how can I do this? I try to get into my work, but then my phone is dinging, my watch is buzzing, and Outlook "flies" a little snippet of every email across my screen. How can I not notice it when notifications assault me in every which way all day long?!

Easy. Turn off your dings and notifications. All of them. Right now. Yes, stop reading and go do it. On your phone, watch, and home computer. Then, when you get into your office, turn them off on your work computer too.

Still terrified? If you have an assistant, tell them what you are doing. Have them run interference for you where they can, and have them be your accountability buddy. Still terrified? Set up an auto-response to run daily, stating that you spend the first X hours each morning in deep intensive work that requires your full concentration. (More often than not, the people on the other end, while perhaps annoyed for a hot second, will also respect the hell out of you and your boundaries, wish they could do the same, and then come to you for advice. Do me a favor: drop me a note when that happens!). In that email, tell them that you spend from X time to Y time each day checking emails and that you will endeavor to have a response to them in Z hours.

Disclaimer: If your boss expects you to be on the ready to respond to any email within five minutes, it may be that you need to have a conversation with them about what you are planning to do and why. If they don't believe you, point them to this article[21] explaining how interrupting you can cause you to lose your focus for twenty-three minutes. That is 5% of an eight-hour workday! To drive this point home even more, if you are interrupted an average of once an hour, you have lost 8 x 23 minutes = 184 minutes. 184 minutes/480 minutes = 38%. That means when you get distracted at least once an hour, you are losing a *third* of your day. A *third* of your focus!

Note that I am not telling you to *never* check your email. I am telling you that there is a time and place and that you get to decide.

Time Management Step 4: Running List

Next up, how do you organize all of the projects and assignments you have in the hopper? Are they on different to-do lists all over your desk, in your purse, or shoved into your lunch bag? How do you know which thing to do first? Do you find yourself rewriting your list over and over, trying to rank it . . . and then realize that all of your time has been spent on composing the damn list and never actually working on it?

Enter my most favorite online invention ever (outside of Pinterest): Trello. The integral piece of why Trello works is that, in just a few minutes of playing around with a Trello board, you end up with a simple visual of what is on your plate, the ranking order of what needs

---

21. Sara Kipler, "Twenty-Three Minutes," getAbstract, updated February 8, 2023, https://journal.getabstract.com/en/2022/03/17/twenty-three-minutes/.

to get done, and what you have accomplished already. Because Trello is an online tool, you can pick it up anywhere: from your laptop, your home office, or work. No longer do you need to worry about leaving your list at home or at work; it is always accessible, even from your phone! The added beauty of Trello is that it allows you to drag around and reorder your to-do lists with ease.

Even though she fought me on it at first, Lo loves Trello. One of her assignments was to go through every list, scrap of paper, file, email, and note to herself and to assemble a master to-do list of all of her projects. Each time she added a new assignment to her Trello board, her sense of control deepened. She started to see how she could get out of the hole. Interestingly, she discovered that she actually had completed more of her tasks than she realized. She just didn't have a method for seeing them all in one place.

Once every blessed thing was in Trello, she finally felt like she could breathe. An added beauty? She noticed that there were a lot of tasks that didn't need her special brain and were better delegated to a newer associate. Now that she could see them, she could delegate them. We worked together to help her get out of being the number one bottleneck at work and transformed her into a mentor and delegator.

Now that you know what Trello did for Lo, you can see why I am obsessed with this tool and teach it to my clients who need help getting their arms around (and their eyes on) their growing to-do lists. You can also see why I encourage the managing partners of law firms to implement Trello boards so that, at a glance, they can see where each case is in active litigation. I also encourage anyone with an assistant to use Trello to communicate tasks to one another, rather than relying on email after email. Emails get accidentally read and lost (and you already know how I feel about the dinging). With a system like Trello, you can load up all of the things you need your assistant to do and then they will have them right there, in an organized list in front of them, ranked in terms of priority.

In addition to Trello being helpful for work, it can be beneficial in other ways as well. I have a board devoted to my home to-do list and a board to organize my gift-giving around the holidays, and I even use it for trip itineraries (it is currently saving my life and sanity as I use it to plan our family's trip to Italy and a Mediterranean cruise). The possibilities are endless.

If you need to organize anything and see it in a way that will just "click" in your brain, I encourage you to try out Trello. I include a sample Trello board in the sparkle & GRIT online resources as an added bonus.

Making the Best of It

Maybe you don't love your job. Maybe you hate thinking about it so much that you don't want to spend one second figuring out how to improve upon it because if you do, then you will feel all the more stuck. If we were to work together, we would dream up all of the possibilities of what is out there for you. I would help you with the mindset you need to get to that new place, and then help you create baby-step homework where we can see if your dream of leaving is more of a reality than you realize it is. (It usually is.) I also get that even if you are unhappy, it feels like it is impossible to leave, and you still make the choice to stay. That is 100% your choice. You get to make the decision; I am going to leave you with a few ideas for shifting your thoughts.

1) If you aren't totally itching to get out of your job and it pays well and allows you to fund your everyday life and fundamental

139

desires—like travel, going out to eat, shopping, paying for your kids' dance and club soccer and your designer purse habit—try a mindset shift. Think about your job this way:

My job allows me to do the things I want to do. Even though it is not my dream, it lets my off time be as pretty damn close to my dream life as I could want. It is enough.

2) If you have a side hustle or project that requires some funding—for example, you need to hire a book editor, you are paying to host a website, you are purchasing products to help get your Etsy store up and running, you need to hire a coach, or you are in the early stages of starting a new business, before it is making you money—then it is likely that your nine-to-five job is funding your dream project. That job is the number one investor in the new you. How about:

Even though this job is driving me bananas, it is a means to an end. My job is giving me a paycheck, health insurance, networking opportunities, and the stability I need to figure out what I really want to do. My early mornings, nights, and weekends are for me to dream and work on my passion project, and my work during the week affords me the ability to do this without feeling desperate for cash as I make my dream job a thing.

3) If you are showing up as a miserable bitch to everyone and cannot give anyone at work the time of day, how is that working out for you? I know you are so freaking miserable. But also, is it really fair to make everyone else around you miserable as well?

Either you need to get the heck out of there, pronto, before you become a person you don't recognize anymore . . . or we have got to get you turned around with your outlook, and fast.

I realize I don't like who I am becoming, and I am a mess. I am sick and tired of waking up miserable that I have to go into work, and I'm sick and tired of scowling at everyone who looks at me. I am going to give myself the gift of solid effort in looking for a new job.

or

I really don't need to be this level of an asshole. I can appreciate the good parts of this job. I can stop taking my shit out on everyone. I can make an effort to find a coworker to have lunch with and can ask her about her life and her day. I can find a new sense of purpose here.

GRIT-work

GRIT-work in this phase is a multipart process. We're going to need your phone, your calendar, and your **GRIT-workbook**. First, put down this book, pick up your phone, and turn off your dings and emails. Go do the same on your computer (don't check emails). What other electronic devices need to be silenced? Go on, do it.

Come back to the book once you've finished.

The next part of **GRIT-work** in this phase requires implementation at work and is in the actual *doing* of this new way of life.

Go ahead right now and schedule a reminder in your phone and on your work calendar that, before you dive into work without a map, you will first take a few moments to decide on your top three tasks/projects. Keep this as a recurring reminder/alarm/notification until it becomes a habit.

Now, how are you going to remind yourself that are in charge of your day (not all those emails!). I encourage a sticky note on your screen saying, "I am the CEO of my day!"

Finally, I want you to schedule in fifteen minutes on your calendar to play around with Trello and see if it is an option for you. (I give you a link to a Trello board example in the sparkle & GRIT resources!)

In summary, this is what you are beginning this week:

1) Top three things: Each morning, decide what three things you will do that day at work.

2) Turn off dings and emails.

3) Trello: Explore Trello and see if it is an option for you.

CHAPTER 8
Make New Friends . . .
But Do You Really Need to Keep the Old?

"Count on Me," Bruno Mars

Women thrive, grow, and sparkle with connection and friendship gone right. In the words of Beyoncé, "I love my husband, but it is nothing like a conversation with a woman that understands you."[22] And, on the converse, when you are stuck in a toxic friendship or surrounded by "mean girls," it can feel like you are back in middle school, and more often than not, you end up feeling like garbage about yourself. All because of the company you surround yourself with.

As you start to grow and become the person you know you are capable of being, your friends are going to notice. Some will cheer you on and jump up and down for you at every turn and will be so insanely interested in you and what is happening in your life that you will notice they will start to make some sparkly new changes as well. When you least expect it, they will mail you a card telling you that you are kicking butt. Others will ignore all of the newness, make fun of it, complain that you have changed, or all of a sudden start to compete with you

---

22. *Beyoncé: Life Is but a Dream*, directed by Ed Burke, Beyoncé Knowles, and Ilan Benatar (2013).

in some strange way. Do you see how it is impossible not to include a friendship chapter in a personal development book when your friend circle has the power to lift you up more than you ever thought possible, or to tank every single one of your ideas before you have a chance to take a baby GRITTY step?

Friends have been a core part of my being throughout my entire life. Growing up, I counted my friends as my family. I was about eleven years old when my parents each remarried with what I considered to be breakneck speed. I quickly went from being the center of the universe as an only child to feeling like an awkward squeaky third wheel in two homes. I was profoundly lonely, not only as the new kid in a new neighborhood in a new school, but at home too. My mom was no longer fully "mine," and my fifth-grade self felt like my stepdad and I were in a competition for her time and love. As for my dad, I only saw him every other weekend, when we holed up at my stepmother's home, which, as nicely as my dad and my stepmother tried to treat me, was just not my *home*. Thus, not only was it developmentally appropriate that my friends became my everything throughout middle school and high school, but it was magnified by the fact that I didn't feel like I fit into my family anymore either.

I learned at an early age how incredibly important it is to cultivate certain friendships. But, over time, I also realized the equal importance of letting go of friends who no longer "fit."

(As an aside, looking back, it is really weird to realize I am now older than my parents were when all of this was going down, which means I am fuller of forgiveness and clarity and able to walk around in their shoes and look at myself, the whiny, tantrum-y, sad, prepubescent fifth grader in a way that I never have before, but that is a story for another book, *Letters to Little Wendy*, to be written and released when the time is right.)

In this chapter, we are going to do a friendship assessment, see what holes you need to fill in the friendship/community department and help you make a conscious effort to stop investing in relationships that are no longer serving you (understanding that some friendships are still important to keep, even when such little time is available to cultivate them in the here and now). We are also going to check in and see if you are being a good friend to the people you love the most.

We have all experienced friendships going from "super hot" to "super cold." We have experienced friendship breakups, misunderstandings, finding new interests, and drifting apart. The quest for true friends doesn't just end at eighteen—it is ongoing as we change, move, and especially as our kids reach new milestones. Friendship is a big deal, and it is not a subject we talk about enough and with the openness it needs and deserves. We spend so much time focusing on work and family that friendship can be an afterthought when really we, especially as women, need friendship to survive. We need friendship to breathe.

Don't worry—I am not going to tell you to break up with your friends tomorrow. I will leave your decisions about what you need to do up to you. Start to evaluate where you spend your time, with whom, and how these people make you feel. Remember that friendship is a two-way street, and you have a choice on how much effort, time, and love you pour into a friendship.

GRIT-work

Pick up your **GRIT-workbook** and let's get to work on your friendship assessment.

1) List the three people who you talk to the most.

Now, for each person you listed, I want you to close your eyes and remember your last few conversations and get-togethers. What did you talk about? Did you laugh? Were you able to get a word in? Did you feel guarded or at ease? As you remember what you talked about, how are you feeling? Can you name that feeling? Where in your body is it coming up for you? Are you surprised by your answer? Is it a good surprise, or are you feeling a little sad?

Jot down as much as you can.

If you are struggling here, I will give you an example.

I am thinking about my friend Susie Q. Every time we chat, we end up gossiping about people we knew maybe ten to twenty years ago. We never seem to talk about anything else. I feel it in the pit of my stomach, and it makes me want to vomit. I am also tired when I get off the phone with her. I feel depleted. While I laughed when we were chatting and poking fun, I am starting to wonder if I am also all those awful things we said about all those other girls. If I can think those thoughts about others, I can think them about myself, and—oh gosh—this sucks.

I am disappointed because we used to have so much fun, but when I think about it, all of that fun was twenty years ago, and we were usually wasted. Hmm.

2) Now, do you have any people in your life who you wish you saw more? Maybe when you're with these people, the energy feels sky-high, and you don't run out of things to talk about, and you just wish you had more time? Who would those people be?

146

List three.

Close your eyes and remember your last few conversations or interactions with these folks. How did it feel when you ran into one another? What did you talk about? Did you laugh? What was the energy level? Did time go by slowly or lightning fast? Did you get to talk at all? Did you feel guarded or at ease? As you remember what you talked about, how are you feeling? Can you name that feeling? Where in your body is it coming up for you? Are you surprised by your answer?

Jot down as much as you can.

Example:

> *I am thinking about my friend Carolyn. Even though I don't see her nearly enough, she is just pure sunshine! Every time we run into one another, we can barely stop talking. There is never a pause in the conversation, and we each go on and on about our gratitude for the other. When I think of her, a big smile pops up on my face, and I feel it in my cheeks. It makes me just want to smile harder. I feel so at ease with her, and it is so funny because in some ways we barely know each other. I just wish I got to spend more time with her.*

After doing these two exercises, what is coming up for you? Rather than going around and breaking up with anyone from the first exercise, think about every interaction with Susie Q as a choice. If you would rather see her in a group setting, suggest that. If you need to decline an invitation to dinner, then do so. If you don't want to chat on the phone because that is when she goes into her vent session, then figure out other ways to talk. Or maybe it *is* time to break up, and that is okay too.

Then go back and think about someone you wished you spent more time with. Make a note in your phone or calendar to remind yourself to send her a text, ask her to go out to dinner next week, or see if she wants to go for a walk. Chances are that she is wanting more time with you too.

As I said in the beginning of this chapter, this is not the time for rash decisions. It is just a check-in. We have so very little free time; make sure you are spending it with people who light you up and don't drag you down. As you spend time with friends, do a check-in before, during, and after. Become self-aware and ask how you are feeling when you are in the presence of your Susie or your Carolyn. Take note. Start to accept or decline invites accordingly, and with grace.

The Old Friends You Need to Hold Close

There is something to be said about a friend who you don't see often enough, but whenever you are together in real life, everything just clicks. I know these friendships can be hard because you want more—and make it a point to ask for more—but perhaps the friend in question just doesn't have it in her to be more. That doesn't mean she doesn't love you or appreciate you. She is just tapped out. These are the friends we cherish, send grace, and keep in our hearts. At the same time, it is also okay to venture out and make new friends who do have more time and availability. But don't get rid of the person who truly gets you just because you are in a period where time is just harder to come by.

My friend like this? My first ever true BFF, Lauren. Lauren and I became super close in seventh grade, when we had both been recently cast to the outskirts of our middle school "groups." When we met during winter swim team, everything just clicked. It was easy to be her friend.

It was fun. I felt like I had found my person, and we were like glue every weekend, every snow day, every life event. We were inseparable through the rest of middle school, through all the boyfriends, through high school, different colleges, different states, med school, law school, all of it. In our twenties, Lauren moved to Colorado for her residency, and I stayed home in Maryland. Still, we kept up the friendship. It looked different and was "less," but the love was still there.

You can imagine the joy I felt in our mid-thirties when I found out Lauren was moving back to Maryland. I was getting my BFF— my person—back! I mentally started planning all of the family get-togethers and outings. I told my husband that our lives were about to change. I came up with a plan where we would see each other every month and just alternate whose house we would go to. I was giddy with excitement! Mind you, all of this was planned out in my head, but we had never actually had this conversation. And then, well, it didn't quite work out that way.

Lauren is a doctor. She's on call on the weekends. Her kids are heavily involved in sports. And our homes are still an hour and a half apart. Over the course of the next two years or so, it became clear that my hopes and dreams for our kids to become BFFs just like we were and for our families to act as one family unit weren't going to happen. And I was mad. I was resentful. I was frustrated and hurt. Yet, every time we *did* get to see each other and every time we *did* talk on the phone, there was always, *always* something she said that was so dead-on and insightful that it reminded me of who I was (in all good ways) and took me back in time to when we were teenagers and it felt like it was us against the world. At each turn, I was like, *Wow, this person really knows me. She really loves me.*

As my kids got older and my weekends became fuller, my desire to hop in a car for ninety minutes waned. My frustration at our friendship dissipated. Somewhere along the way, I also had the epiphany that Lauren had not signed up for the expectations I had cast upon her when I had found out she was moving back. I realized I had been unfair. As time went on, I "got" where she was coming from more and more. Her lack of desire to trek and come to visit and take the kids away from their activities and friend groups made sense. For Lauren, our lack of seeing each other had nothing to do with how she felt about me, and it didn't take away from the incredible friendship we had that carried us through some pretty major milestones that occurred in our teens and twenties. My heart forgave. When I was able to look at our friendship through a new lens, I realized I hadn't lost her; I just needed to understand what path of the journey we were both on. We were both in the thick of it, and we were both 100% where we need to be most of the time: with our families. No longer am I in a place where I need to substitute friends for family, which is what I relied on her to be for a really long time. Lauren and I are in a new stage of our friendship, and that is okay. It works.

GRIT-work

It is time to continue with our friendship assessment and lean into the idea of old friends. This one can be emotionally hard and challenging. Go easy on yourself. Get out the tissues if you need to. A good cry can really help sometimes. Allow yourself to write away in your **GRIT-workbook**.

Who is your version of Lauren? Who is an old friend you still need to keep close?

Take a minute; breathe her in. How are you feeling? Do you feel loving? Wistful? A little mournful or sad, but still complete in a weird way? How do you feel when you extend her some grace? When you imagine yourselves on the phone? When you see her and it has been months or years?

So long as she doesn't make you feel like Susie does, so long as the times you do get to share with her are good, don't throw her away. Even if she doesn't 100% get the "you" you are today, she loves you deeply and knows your history better than anyone else, and that cannot be re-created. She knows so many versions of you, and through them all, she loves you. Give her time, give her space, but also give her love and acceptance. Give her grace. And give yourself some grace too. You are allowed to mourn that the friendship is now different. Now is the time to reimagine it. Reimagine it and repurpose it in a way that feels good to you. So long as she loves you for you, she is a keeper.

If you are the friend who never has time for that old friend in your life, cherish the friend who is patiently waiting for you. Admire her for the stamina for the friendship the two of you hold and be grateful that she is out there, waiting for a time when you both are ready, cheering you on, and also loving all of the many versions of you she has seen you grow into over the last thirty years.

Community Mindset

One of the hardest things that happens when you start to grow and live the sparkle & GRIT mindset is that some of your friends will no longer "get" you. Your sparkle will begin to grow and shine bright. You will feel more alive and like you than ever before. Your face will change. Your voice will change. Your outlook will change. You will be sick of the old way. Some people in your life will ask, "Why are you changing? Why do you need to be different? Isn't the old life just fine?" Don't be surprised by a new wave of loneliness. Even if you are inviting your friends to jump in the water with you, they might decide to stay put on the pool deck. When you go from a life of different shades of gray to technicolor, you want everyone else to "get it" too. You want to shake everyone and say, "Don't you see? Life just got so much better because _____ [fill in the blank]. I want this for you too!"

More often than not, and as much as you want it for them because you love and care about them and want them to "wake up" and get to be all sparkly with you, your friends don't want it. They aren't ready, and this is their choice, not yours.

Consider this. Your friends who aren't jumping in with you might just see themselves as losing their friend. Give them grace. It is not our job to "change them." You can hold space and be there for them when they are ready.

One of my favorite sayings is "A rising tide lifts all boats," which I also take to mean "Boats in a harbor rise and fall together." It is time for you to find a harbor that works better for you. As the sparkle grows, it is imperative that you connect with like-minded individuals. sparkle & GRIT is a community mindset. You don't have to do it alone. You show up every day, not just for yourself but for that other woman out there who is also ready to shine and *do*.

How? Given that we are all about boats and harbors, let's go back and find your anchor from chapter 5. Surely there is a group of people out there who have the same passions as you, love the same thing, and are right there in your community or perhaps right there and waiting for you online. It is your duty to find them, reach out, message, and connect. Go to the event, pop on the Zoom call, try out a new class. Over time, in ways you cannot even imagine right now, your community will become your rock. I promise you, your harbor is out there. There is a slip calling your name, waiting for you to pull up and dock, waiting for that crazy tide to come in and raise you and your new friends up so high that you could not imagine ever having gone through this crazy thing called life without them.

My proof? My Fab 5. Anchored first in sweat. If you had told me just a few years ago that I would have the most incredible group of friends who get me to my core, lift me up when I am hiding under my covers, and celebrate my wins on a daily basis with pure love and joy, I don't think I would have believed you. Yet, here we are.

Katie and I were good friends and ran the 4x800 together our junior and senior years of high school. We reconnected in our thirties due to our mutual love of fitness and getting back in shape. Because we were always doing the same workout programs at the same time, loved to cook, and had kids of similar ages, we easily fell into friendship again. A year or so later, her college friend, Donna, joined us. Similar story: loved to work out, had children, and had a zest for life and telling it like it was. I fell in friendship love with her. A year or so after that, an old college acquaintance, someone I barely knew back in my F&M (go Fummers!) days, Karis, kept commenting on my Facebook posts, and we started to have conversations about working out, kids, our work with children, and our careers in therapy and family law. We also fell into friendship hard and fast and never stopped running out of things to talk about and discovering new similarities we shared. Around the same time, I randomly friend requested a law mom, Jackie, out in Colorado because she looked cool and nice and normal, I love Colorado, and we had similar law interests. Before I knew it, we also fell into a deep friendship, bonding over everything "law mom," collaborated on ways we could each expand our growing mediation practices, and turn to each other frequently for advice on a deep soul level that not everyone gets.

Going into 2020 and the pandemic, I was friends with these four, but on separate message threads and chats. In March 2020, when the world was going to hell in a handbasket, I decided to throw us all together into one chat on one app called Marco Polo, and voilà, the rest is history. Our bond grew fast and deep. Just like that group I found in tenth grade, we all just "fit." Words cannot do what we have justice. This level of friendship was the missing piece for so many years. We all have a place now where we are 100% truly "gotten." On days we don't feel that way and feel like one of us doesn't "get it," we aren't shy about saying that either—with love.

We are three years strong into about two hours of chatting a day, a text thread that starts to blow up at 5 a.m. every morning, a Facebook message thread, and an Instagram one as well. We are in constant contact. We have cried big fat ugly tears to one another. We have laughed our heads off. We have had epic dance parties. These women were the first to come and visit me and take care of me (from Colorado, New Hampshire, North Carolina, and New Jersey) after my hysterectomy. They are the first to pick me up and the last to let me down. If I can find my ride-or-die crew as I enter my forties, so can you. You just need to be open to looking. We would not be what we have today if we each didn't go out on a limb and be open to chatting with someone new and unexpected. The key here is to be open to any possibility. You have no way of knowing who will be in your harbor until you take action. Take a GRITTY step of reaching out to an old friend or commenting on an acquaintance's post. Strike up a conversation. Go out on a limb. Your Fab 5 is within reach and waiting for you to take the first step.

How to Be a Good Friend

This section could be a whole book, but there are some universal truths when it comes to friendship.

1) Your friend might change. Love her anyway.
2) A good friend is not someone who talks behind your back. Don't talk about her behind her back. If you have something to say to her, extend her the courtesy of telling it to her face, with grace.
3) Even if you are so busy you cannot see straight, text your friend that you love her. If you know your friend is so busy she cannot see straight, text her that you love her and that she has this!
4) Your friend's kids and your kids might not get along. Love her anyway. (And love her kids too.)
5) Don't be a flake. If you have plans to meet up but are tired and would rather hang out on the couch and watch TV, get your butt up and go hang out. Do not cancel on her. That plan you are about to cancel could be the lifeline she has been looking forward to all week.
6) If your friend goes through a major life event—death, divorce, layoff—get off your ass and be there for her. Even if you have to inconvenience yourself.
7) Make sure you give her time and listen. If you need to take up a lot of space in a conversation with her because your life is exploding, signal that to her. Let her know at the beginning of the conversation and make sure she is in a space to hear it. Also

make sure she has time to talk and vent in your conversation as well. Listening and vocalizing are two-way streets.

8) Forgive her. She is human.

9) Apologize when you screw up and don't expect her to tell you "it is all okay." Truth is, it wasn't okay, and that doesn't mean she doesn't still love you. She loves you in spite of your screwups. Be okay with that.

10) You might change. Love your friend anyway.

GRIT-work

This chapter is not intended to inspire you to start axing friends right away. Be curious and be aware. Audit how you are feeling as you chat with friends on the phone, read through message threads, see someone out for dinner, etc. When it feels right, or when you are struggling with a certain friendship, open your **GRIT-workbook** and find the section on friendship. Plug in and do the work. Be intentional. Consider saying no to the next hangout, and evaluate how that makes you feel. Consider leaving that group chat of women you befriended at the start of the pandemic, the one that felt good at first but now just feels catty and off-putting. In each instance, check in, feel the feels. Do you want more or less? You are the best guide here.

Concentrate on growth. Who was someone you listed who you want to see more of, someone like my Carolyn? Can you make a commitment to reach out to her by the end of this month and plan a get together? Ask her to go for a walk, hike, or cup of coffee?

Think about your old friend, your OG BFF. Think of where you can extend grace or where you can show up differently and in a way that works for you both.

Finally, find your community. Who lights you up? What do you love to do or discuss the most? If it is fitness, perhaps the answer is a local running club or gym or an online accountability group. If it is politics, consider volunteering to be an election judge or joining a campaign team. If it is sewing, consider finding a local sewing group with meetups and get-togethers. Your people are out there. As always, check in with yourself after each gathering. How are you feeling? Do you want more? If so, then go again. Find a friend, get to know her better. If you feel weird but are still curious about it, maybe try one more time, and if it is still a no, keep looking. You will find your people. It may be that the best is yet to come.

CHAPTER 9

What's Health Got to Do with Pencil Erasers, Dance Floors, CEOs & Anxiety?

"Survivor," Destiny's Child

Pencil Erasers

A humiliating experience at the OB-GYN almost cost me my life.

Okay, that is a little dramatic and over-the-top. But hear me out. It easily could have.

In 2008, I had my first abnormal Pap. The full story can be found on my original blog.[23] Long story short, HPV was the culprit, and after a colposcopy and a LEEP, my lady parts were "healthy" again. Enter a *huge* sigh of relief and an effort to get pregnant ASAP (which only took three long years).

Now fast-forward to 2014. After my daughter was born, I returned to my midwives for an annual checkup. I remember being surprised and

23. Wendy S. Meadows, "Paps, Colpos, LEEPS—Oh My!" Lawfully Lean, April 23, 2021, https://lawfullylean.com/2021/04/23/paps-colpos-leeps-oh-my/.

a little shocked when they didn't give me a Pap. My midwife kindly told me that the experts had changed the guidelines and I only needed a Pap every three years.

"Even with my history?"

"Yup," and I was dismissed.

That didn't feel right to me. I was also really bummed because I *loved* this woman. She did an amazing job delivering my babies, and I trusted her. But this did not sit right.

When it was time to go back for an annual exam, I didn't feel like I had any choice but to switch doctors, and I found a GYN whose website said he dealt with women like me who had encountered abnormal Paps, had LEEPs, etc. I assumed this new doc would be a good fit because he was under the same medical group as my surgeon in case the "Stage 0" cancer came back (which it did, but again, a story already told in a blog[24]).

I didn't expect this annual exam to be different from any other. But this one will always and forever stick out in my mind. To set the scene, I need to go back and put myself in my July 2014 body. I was still breastfeeding. I was exhausted because my little girl was only sleeping for a max of four hours, ever. I was holding weight on my body that I never had before. I felt frumpy and was still wearing the cheap and in-between-size stretchy work pants I had picked up at Express to help transition from my pregnancy body to my old prepregnancy clothes.

Per the usual in these situations, I was lying down, stripped naked, with just a gown on. I remember the doc opening my gown, preparing to do the breast exam. I was terrified that my milk would let down and squirt him in the face despite an epic pumping session right before the

---

24. Wendy S. Meadows, "My Hysterectomy Story," Lawfully Lean, July 24, 2021, https://lawfullylean.com/2021/07/24/my-hysterectomy-story/.

exam to prevent such a crazy embarrassing event. Luckily, that didn't happen.

Something worse did. He messed with my mind.

He looked down at me and my pencil-eraser nipples as I lay exposed on the exam table and said, "Wow, you must be really cold" in this weird, off-putting, jokey tone.

I have no idea what words actually came out of my lips. I doubt I said anything. I remember thinking,

Really dude?

REALLY?!

You are a freaking OB-GYN who SHOULD be fully aware of all of the different ways a woman's breasts change, especially when she is BREASTFEEDING and her kid's goal is literally to suck the life out of her! Of course her nipples are going to be long and stick out!

Yet, instead of feeling empowered or ready to take him on, I went from being proud of my breasts for nourishing my baby to feeling ashamed, weird, and like my boobs must look wrong. What's worse? Despite my history, despite me having already advocated for myself to fight for the Pap, it took me two years to have the courage to find and schedule with a new GYN after that appointment. *Two years.* What if the cancer had come back in those two years? What if this man had scarred me so badly that I just never went back? Ever?

Those what-ifs have some real-deal consequences.

Just several years after the fiasco with Dr. Creepy, because I was able to find a new GYN I trusted, because I took it upon myself to remind the doctors that because of my history I need a yearly Pap, I discovered that the carcinoma adenoma in situ was back. Before it could get worse, I had a hysterectomy, which very well may have saved me from developing full-fledged cervical cancer. What if I hadn't, though? What if my embarrassment had kept me from ever visiting an OB-GYN again? What if I had been so worried about what my boobs looked like and what a doc might say to me that I was also scared off of mammograms? Scary, right?

How many women has this happened to who did not have the courage to go back?

I am happy to report that, through immersing myself in self-love, coupled with years of humor foisted upon me by my very spunky and outspoken daughter, I have grown to love my super-long, pencil-eraser-sized nipples, which she lovingly and laughingly calls my "stick boobies." Each time we laugh, it helps me chip away at the Dr. Creepy memory and replace it with my funny, well-meaning, silly daughter's smiling face.

Let my pencil-eraser-sized nipples be your reminder that

1) You need to advocate for the services you need,
2) You should not let one creepy, crappy experience keep you from getting the medical care you deserve, and
3) Just like you are the CEO of your day, as we talked about in chapter 7, you are also the CEO of your health.

GRIT-work

What doctor appointment have you been putting off? Remember, we cannot treat what we don't know. Your annual? Your mammogram? Your colonoscopy? Your dermatologist appointment? I could go on and on. It is time to get those appointments booked. Break out your calendar and block out an hour to do the following:

1) Book an annual physical. Ask about getting your bloodwork done beforehand so you can actually discuss your results *during*

your appointment and get all of your questions answered, as opposed to waiting until after your appointment to get your blood tested and having to ask all of your questions in an after-visit portal. If you don't like your doc (like my Dr. Creepy), ask around and find a new one.

2) Book your mammogram (guidelines call for forty or over).

3) Book your Pap.

4) Book your colonoscopy (guidelines call for forty-five or over).

5) Book your dermatologist checkup.

6) Who else do you need to see? Book that too.

7) If you have been to a jillion docs and no one is listening to you or giving you what you need, consider something outside of the box. You are the CEO. Explore your options. Use your Google search bar. See what speaks to you. For me, chiropractor and acupuncture visits have worked wonders. I have friends who swear by Reiki. I have had friends seek out physicians trained in functional medicine and have seen their health do a 360. You need to remember that no one else is going to do this for you.

Dance Floors

Raise your hand if it is hard for you to say no to a third or fourth glass of wine when you have already had two. Raise your hand if you sometimes drink too much for no good reason, beat yourself up in the morning, and ask yourself, *Why on earth did I NEED to do that?* It took me until I was forty-three years old (yes, this year) to figure out why I would go for the third or fourth cocktail/glass of sauv blanc/what have you. It turns out that I have been on a twenty-one-year-long mission to find the dance party.

Give me a minute; you will see what I mean.

First, let's go back to 1998. I had been a "good kid" for pretty much all of high school. Like most high schools, ours was divided into groups and cliques, but there was no group or clique that was better than the others; we all just "were." This wasn't by accident—this was by design for our area. Our small city ensured that each community within our city and each high school had a diverse population in terms of socioeconomics, race, religion, and creed and that we should all be celebrated, we all were accepted, we all mattered. Neat, huh? And it also sort of sounds like the beginning of a teen dystopian fiction novel, doesn't it? Well, close. I grew up in a planned community, Columbia, Maryland, where the whole intent of our city, built in 1967, was to foster a community where acceptance ran first and foremost. Columbia was designed to be a city that encouraged and promoted "economic, racial, and cultural harmony."[25]

How does this translate to being a high school kid? I am not sure if it was because I grew up in Columbia, but my high school experience didn't match what is shown on the mainstream TV shows or movies you see now (does anyone's?). As far as I am aware, there were no raging parties that everyone in the school was dying for an invite to. There was no underdog "dorky" kid trying to make their way into said parties to then have the quarterback fall head over heels in love with them. Sure, there was some bullying, and not everyone bought into the whole kumbaya vibe that Columbia has to offer, but my high school was missing the hierarchy of "cool" that you so often see depicted by the entertainment industry. My ride-or-die group of friends had no peer pressure to party it up. Instead of sneaking bottles of alcohol from our

25. Jimmy Stamp, "James W. Rouse's Legacy of Better Living Through Design," *Smithsonian Magazine*, April 23, 2014, https://www.smithsonianmag.com/history/james-w-rouses-legacy-better-living-through-design-180951187/.

parents' liquor cabinets on Saturday nights, we would hole up in each other's basements, and we found it hilarious when we put on "brown-bag skits" (literally, you throw about five items in a brown paper grocery bag, hand it to the team, and they have ten minutes to make up a skit with the items). We were campy, in love with one another, and comfortable enough in our own skin and with each other that we didn't need any help in the form of liquid courage.

I graduated from high school forgetting what it was like not to fit in anywhere. Freshman year of college, everything changed.

All of a sudden, parties became the central point of all social gatherings. There was no sobriety on the weekends (or even on Wednesdays, for that matter). In just a few weeks, us college freshmen were well-versed in what fraternity parties were held on what night (I can still tell you) and what type of free drinks they would have (e.g., go to Skull on Friday night and expect to see a vat of "Purple Motherfuckers," which I am pretty sure was just grain alcohol and grape Gatorade). As first-semester freshman women, there were no barriers to the parties we could get into.

But just because we all "got in" doesn't mean we all *fit* in.

I went from my hunky-dory planned community and old-soul friendships to a college filled with students who were better-dressed, smarter, richer, more experienced, and organized into systems and hierarchies of frats and sororities. Not only did I not feel cool enough, but I was told so explicitly when I didn't get into the two sororities I made a bid for my freshman year. Something about me, Wendy, just wasn't good enough.

How did I cope? I partied it up.

Before I go on, I need to write a note to my friends who are in recovery, sober, or sober-curious. I am betting you already know the stuff that comes in the rest of this chapter and then some. If any of this is going to feel triggering to you in any way, please feel free to skip it. But to my friends who are scared to read this section because you either know you are dependent upon alcohol or you are afraid of what I am going to suggest, I gently encourage you to read it anyway and, if there is a nudge that you need to get some more help, then *do* so. Without shame. Some of my dearest friends are in recovery. They are taking the steps they need to take to live their best lives and show up 100% to their families. Their strength and courage is admirable. Seriously, making that decision and then announcing to others—and then perhaps even the world—that you have a dependency "problem" is one of the most brave and vulnerable acts there is.

Back to fall of 1998 Wendy. What did I do about my growing insecurities?

A bunch of Miller Lite, Yuengling if I knew the older frat brothers who kept the good kegs behind the bar, and purple MF'ers on Friday nights.

My favorite part about going out on a Friday or Saturday night? Losing myself completely—my inhibitions, my racing mind, my worries that I wasn't smart enough, cool enough, rich enough—and leaving it all there on a kick-ass dance floor.

It was easy to fit in when you were in those crowded, sticky, tiled, dark, dank, small spaces. Losing myself in the music, feeling it sway through my body, screaming lyrics with the whole dance floor, grinding it out with who knows who. The dance floor was the great equalizer, it was *fun*, all of my inhibitions melted away. I felt beautiful, sexy, and seen on the dance floor. I felt connection when my body just knew how to dance with someone I had just met. Twirling, eye contact, laughing, sweating, moving just right. The dance floor was my everything.

But I didn't do it sober. I drank to prepare for the dance floor. I drank so my mind could let loose and let my body move to the beat with zero worries. I drank so I could forget about all the ways I didn't fit in and have liquid courage to be in rooms where I didn't know if I belonged or not. I drank because I was looking for the dance party where I felt like I could just truly really be the essence of *me*, and if that was "too much" for anyone, well, I could point to my red Solo cup as the excuse.

I realized that perhaps I am sometimes still looking for that metaphorical dance party.

When I think about the nights I drink too much and wake up the next morning moaning, thinking, *Why did I DO that?!* I realize that more often than not, I was really just expecting the dance floor to make its way into existence. I was waiting for the moment that things would *turn on* and get lively, and we would all shed any inhibitions and be *alive* and fun. Let loose. Live! Why do I keep on looking for it, when I sure as hell am not going to find *fun* and *aliveness* alone on my couch after watching a Netflix show?

It makes you think, doesn't it? What *is* the point of overdrinking if there is no dance floor—metaphorical or literal? (Or at all, for that matter.) What does it come down to for me? When I feel like I am having fun, I don't want it to stop (yes, I am also an Enneagram Seven). I keep thinking that more fun is just around the corner (that dance party!) and forget that overdrinking will leave me feeling overdrawn and negative in the morning. Once I can examine what I am doing (drinking too much on occasion) and why (looking for *fun*), I can start to change my approach. I can start to have an honest conversation with myself and put up guardrails to ensure I am making good decisions.

So, as much as I love a good glass of wine, a delicious craft cocktail, or a good brewery, I can also admit that, other than alcohol being a fun thing to "do" and a delicious taste to experience, after two drinks, it is often a case of diminishing returns.

Why does it matter? Why am I stressing this point here? Because what you do the night before 100% dictates who you will be the next day. What you consume the night before has a direct correlation to the sparkle you will feel and the GRITTY steps you will have the capacity to take.

We have already covered the importance of not letting clients/work/inbound emails be the CEO of your day. You also just heard me talk about how you need to be the CEO of your health when it comes to proactively scheduling preventive appointments. Here is another one. Are you letting alcohol be the CEO of your day?

Try this on.

You wake up: How do you feel? Is your mouth dry? Nose stuffy? Headache? Foggy? Do you feel disoriented? Unmotivated? Dead damn tired because you barely slept? Still feel buzzed? Groggy? You vow to have no booze until the weekend. You don't need that glass of wine tonight.

Your workout: You skip it. Or you muster up the energy, but you feel like crapola the whole time. Your heart rate is all over the place.

Your workday: Everything feels a bit harder. Your brain isn't working like normal. You are *craving* pizza and an ice-cold Coke with crunchy ice, and you toss your salad in the trash. You munch. And munch. Your to-do list of all the things feels overwhelming. You grab some chocolate and Skittles to get you through. Around 4-ish, you are thinking, *A glass of wine would sure be nice. I know I said I wasn't going to have anything tonight, but maybe I will . . . hmm . . . after all, tomorrow is Friday, and then it will practically be the weekend . . . maybe it is a fine idea after all.*

Home from work: You are tired but also finally starting to wake up. You are in that weird in-between feeling. But your headache is gone and, man, work was stressful. You decide, *Why not?* You pour a glass of wine. Who cares?

Parenting: You notice you are getting a little edgy. Your patience and tolerance for no's, talking back, and all the kid things starts to evaporate. You lose your cool. You pour another half glass. When it is bedtime, you aren't fully present. Bedtime is taking too damn long. Your kiddos are telling you about their days, but you are only half listening. You are thinking about them being asleep so you can go pour another glass and sit in solitude, scrolling social media or watching Netflix. You don't really care; you just want to be left alone.

See how all of *that* stemmed from just two glasses of wine the night before? Do you see how it affects your mood, workout, work, energy, nutrition, and parenting the next day? Do you see how it permeates every blessed thing in your life?

Are you letting alcohol be the CEO of your day? I find that when my weekday alcohol intake increases (and slowly but surely becomes more habit than actual desire), slowly but surely the quality of my days crumbles as well.

I am not here to beat you up about this, nor am I going to blow smoke up your ass. I am simply asking you to check in with yourself, be aware, and make some swaps.

GRIT-work

Open up your **GRIT-workbook** and answer the following prompts:

1) Do I have any alcohol habits now? What are they?
2) Are they serving me?
3) Where can I cut back?
4) What new habit can I form?
5) When am I allowing alcohol to serve as my CEO?
6) When do I notice that alcohol is increasing my anxiety? How does that manifest for me?

If you are stuck trying to figure out a new habit, what about committing to either only having alcohol on weekends or only having two drinks when you go out on Saturday night?

During the course of reading this book, I also want you to think about your alcohol consumption while you are in the moment.

Step 1: Simply notice. What is your alcohol consumption? When you pour a glass of wine, do you even want it? Are you in the mood for it, or is it a habit?

Step 2: What can you commit to today to start limiting your booze intake? Can you give up drinks on weekdays? Cut down to just Friday *or* Saturday? When you decide to go for it, can you commit to a one and done or a two and through? Just try it. You will thank yourself in the morning!

Remember this: Do you remember when our kiddos were babies and all of the baby books said "sleep begets sleep"? Same goes with the booze. The less you drink it, the less you want it. The more, the more. You start popping a bottle every day, that is your new norm, and you might forget that you don't even want it every night.

Sugar

Every single December, around the 17th or so, I suffer the same weird symptoms. I start to burp more. I have acid reflux that reminds me of pregnancy. My anxiety is through the roof, catching me early in the morning and sending me into a hand-wringing panic, and I start biting off the head of anyone in my path. It is not pretty.

And, every December, usually in the afternoon as I go to reach for yet another Christmas cookie and start to feel that weird acid reflux gurgle in my throat almost instantaneously, I say, "Oh yeah, crap. Freaking sugar—*you* are the one making me feel like this! Damn you!"

Every time this happens, I swear off all sugar, candy, and cookies for the next forty-eight hours. In that short period of time, I can feel the anxiety melt away, I sleep better, the acid reflux goes away, and my head starts operating more clearly. Every time. Every time, I also say to myself, *How did I forget this?*

Have you experienced this too?

Sugar is such a weird, funny, sort of awful, sort of wonderful enigma of a thing, isn't it? It is that one thing that universally we hate to love and love to hate. It is the front and center of a celebration and the work of the devil in most nutrition plans.

When I was a kid, sugar was the *world!* I could not wait for Halloween!

When I was a teen, sugar was a treat that I bought with my own money, so it was an indulgence mixed with a bit of pride and a tad of mischief because no one could tell me no, but I also knew my parents would disapprove.

In my college days, sugar was gummy worms and peach rings to help me study and fuel late-night road trips.

In law school, sugar was a helpful tool to keep me awake and help me pay attention. I think I gained about ten pounds in law school just from eating a bag of Skittles a day so that I could feign rapt attention when attempting to learn the definition of "consideration."

What place does sugar have now?

Nowadays, as a parent, sugar is that Halloween candy, sitting high up on a shelf at the top of my pantry where I put the kids' stash to hide it from them, and, let's face it, to make it harder for me to grab. But, when it calls my name so loudly and repeatedly that I simply must pause my late-night TV, get the ladder, and celebrate with the last two peanut butter cups, I know that sugar has once again won.

Haven't we already given sugar too many years of our lives? Too many years to play CEO? Too much time to ramp up our anxiety?

GRIT-work

Open up your **GRIT-workbook** and answer the following prompts:

1) When do I consume sugary things?
2) How do I feel afterward? Physically?
3) Mentally?
4) What new habit can I form?
5) When am I allowing sugar to serve as my CEO?
6) When do I notice that sugar is increasing my anxiety? How does that manifest for me?

If you are stuck on a new habit, how about limiting candy to once a week, replacing the 3 p.m. candy binge with a green apple, or ordering your Starbucks without any pumps of syrup?

Also, just as I asked you to do with increasing your awareness with regard to your alcohol consumption, your **GRIT-work** here is to pay attention. The next time you eat a peanut butter cup (or five), check in, from the bottom of your stomach to all the way to the top of your head. Is your stomach flip-flopping, growling, overly full, hurting? How are your esophagus and throat? Do you feel acid-y? Heartburn-y? Burp-y? Now, here are the weird places to feel it: how are you feeling in the back of and on top of your head? Between your ears? Lately, when I indulge in any sort of sugar, I get this weird whoosh-y feeling swirling inside the top of my head, right above my ears. None of it feels very good, does it? Even the sugar high that gives you a hot second to power through the end of a project doesn't last so long. And then there's the crash and the utter fatigue you feel when the sugar high wears off—how is that good?

I am not telling you to give up all sugar forever and ever; I just want you to be more discerning. To pay more attention and adjust accordingly. Sometimes the best way we can give up something is to realize that there is no part of our body that feels good when we consume it. To be conscious of all the ick feelings that occur. To feel what it is doing to our bodies.

Step 1: Simply notice. How do you feel when you eat sugar? When does it start taking effect? Can you stop at a square of chocolate? Do you go for the whole bar?

Step 2: What do you want to change? Do you need fewer sugary treats in your house? Do you need to walk down a different hall from the vending machine? Do you need to pack an apple or a bell pepper to keep you from raiding the candy bowl down the hall? What *one* swap can you make this week?

Talk to Someone—Outside Help

By now I am hoping you have figured out what pencil erasers, dance floors, CEOs, and anxiety all have in common: your health, of course! While I have found that being on top of my medical appointments and limiting alcohol and sugar works wonders for my anxiety, sometimes it is not enough. There have been time periods when I have enlisted outside help in the form of therapists and coaches to help me deal more intensely with the matter at hand.

In case you haven't heard this yet, there is absolutely *zero* shame in therapy, and I recommend it to my mediation and coaching clients at every turn. You do not need to have "something wrong with you" to go to therapy. That is not what it is for. Therapy is to help you heal, grow, and understand. Therapy mends bridges within you. It can help mend bridges with others. Therapy has given me some of my biggest insights that have totally reframed sticky thoughts and allowed movement and growth. Therapy helps us understand what neural pathways we have developed that are no longer serving us, and it helps us create new ones.

I look at therapy like Oprah giving out prizes on her favorite things episodes: "You get therapy! You get therapy!" Who wouldn't benefit from having a rapt listening ear and a new perspective? Who doesn't want to heal past wounds and finally grow?

If you have been on the fence about finding a therapist, this is your sign.

CHAPTER 10
Parenting Is No Joke

"Good Job," Alicia Keys

If I could ever physically come through a chapter to sit on the couch next to you, give you a hug and a pep talk, and tell you that you are doing a good job, this would be the chapter. The next best thing? Go listen to Alicia Keys, "Good Job." Hear her words pour over you and imagine that she wrote this song just for you and for the exact stage of parenting you are in. If you need a moment to just to sit and cry, let yourself do that.

This song gets me every time. The first time I heard it, I was doing a Peloton ride with Robin mid-pandemic. The words hit me so hard and fast that before I knew it, I was ugly crying and draped over the bike. When a song can capture your exhaustion, see you, and tell you what you need to hear all in one, it is like the perfect meal for your soul.

There are a few statistics I want to share with you as we enter this chapter. I feel two ways about these statistics. On one hand, they are a great wake-up call. Our time with our kids as littles is precious, limited, and fleeting. It makes me so sad—and makes me want to vomit—when I realize that never ever can we get back the babies, toddlers, or pre-tweens. We can't even get back who our kids were just yesterday. That really sucks. On the other hand, the last thing we need is another guilt trip when it comes to parenting. When I see social media encouraging me to step it up because these years are fleeting, I sort of want to punch the "influencer" in the face. Sorry, not sorry. And, at the same time, I do *get* it. I do understand this time is limited and that these reminders are a wake-up call to do my best to enjoy the moment I am in now.

I am going to go out on a limb and share these statistics with you because I think it is important that we are super aware of what we have and how much time we have in the here and now. It is also important that we remember that, whatever stage we are in, "this too shall pass." Perhaps these stats will serve as a relief to you. Or perhaps these numbers will be the kick in the pants you need to shake off your multitasking brain and snap into the present when you are hanging with your kiddo.

1) Seventy-five percent of the time we will spend with our kids in our lifetimes will be spent by the time they turn twelve.[26]
2) Ninety percent of the time we will spend with our kids will have occurred by the time they turn eighteen.[27]

Now, what do we do about this?

26. Ginny Yurich, "75% of the Time We Spend With Our Kids in Our Lifetime Will Be Spent by Age 12," 1000 Hours Outside, accessed July 13, 2023, https://www.1000hoursoutside.com/blog/time-with-kids-before-age-12.

27. Tim Urban, "The Tail End," Wait but Why, December 11, 2015, https://waitbutwhy.com/2015/12/the-tail-end.html.
Tim Denning, "You Don't Have as Long with Your Parents as You Think," Ascent Publication, Medium, March 28, 2019, https://medium.com/the-ascent/you-dont-have-as-long-with-your-parents-as-you-think-57fc081d24cc.
Donn Felker, "Make the Most of Your Time," Donn Felker, accessed July 13, 2023, https://www.donnfelker.com/make-the-most-of-your-time/.

Parenting Is Hard—End Stop, Period

When people tell you that parenting is hard, you automatically assume they are talking about sleepless nights with newborns. Once you get through that stage, you assume they were talking about the terrible twos. After that, the assumption is that they were talking about the teen years, where we are terrified of what experiments our teens will partake in with sex, drugs, and alcohol. After that, the assumption is that they were talking about the stress associated with paying for college tuition.

Yet, as I write this chapter, I am in the midst of the most challenging stage of being a parent. No one warned me about this part. My kiddos are eleven and nine. They are my light. They make me laugh so hard. There are times I feel that they truly "get" me, more than anyone else ever gotten me, and this is a feeling of deep belongingness that I never experienced before them. I feel seen and raw and loved. My kids are growing into their real-deal personalities, are deeply connected to their emotions, and are already smarter or better at certain things than I am. And—I was not prepared for this stage to be as hard as it is. The back-talking, bargaining, reasoning. The struggling with treating your kids like real people with real opinions and real memories and feelings versus taking the role of the authoritative figure becoming exasperated and saying "because I said so." The frustration of trying so hard to do everything right and wanting to do everything for your kids that you felt was missing from your life and yet still feeling like it's not enough. The really hard days when you go to bed whispering with your spouse, asking, "How much did we screw up today?"

As our kids approach their teenage years and we realize that we have already spent half of their childhood lives with them under our roof, the terror is real. Did we not teach them enough? Love them enough? Were we too hard on them? Too lackadaisical? Did we let

177

them eat too much sugar? Allow too much screen time? Did we let them down with all of those ways we said we would do better and try harder? Is it too late to fix it? Will things improve so the four of us can get along again? Will the kids remember all the good things we did? Will our kiddos make some dumb life-threatening decision when they are out and about? Did we teach them the right things? Did we yell too much? Give in too much? Work too much? Use electronics as a crutch when we should have pushed for the hike, despite all the complaining? These questions don't stop and are on a constant B-roll, playing in the backs of our brains. No wonder we are freaking exhausted.

Parenting is universally hard—period. None of us is immune. Even if you see someone with a picture-perfect family on Facebook or Instagram (or whatever the new platform is when you are reading this book), I can promise you there is a story behind the pictures. I have coached women all over the US for years, and I have counseled parents in the state of Maryland since 2005. One universal truth? Parenting is hard at every stage for everyone. Period. End stop.

And . . .

Your kid chose you to be their parent. I 100% believe this. *You* are absolutely the best parent for your kiddo. No one else can do it like you.

Best Family Self

Now that we have established that parenting is hard, we need to take the focus off of our kids and turn the microscope onto ourselves. Some of this will hurt. Remember, it is okay to throw this book across the room and scream. Just pick it back up.

Starting small:

When I look back on my worst parenting days and reflect on where things went awry, I always notice two things. 1) I did not begin my days by asking myself how I could best show up for my family, and 2) I showed up to parenting exhausted, either because I didn't get enough sleep, I watched too much TV, I ate too much sugar, or I felt hungover (and these days, I can feel "hungover" when it is just a glass or two of wine).

The good news? There are easy fixes for these issues, fixes with concrete, GRITTY steps. Let's get to work.

GRIT-work

Time to go get your GRIT-workbook! Find these prompts and answer them:

1) What time each day can I check in with myself and ask what kind of parent I will be today? How will I remind myself? Will I journal it? Say it out loud? Share it with my partner? My kid?
2) What guardrails can I put in place so I am showing up as a CEO in my parenting? What steps do I need to take at night so I am showing up as the parent I need to be tomorrow?

Looking at the big picture:

Once we know we are plugging in each morning and setting an intention to plug into our family, and once we know we have set ourselves up for the rest by giving ourselves enough sleep and enough "me time," we can make time to evaluate the bigger picture when it comes to parenting and how we approach this role. It is time to recognize what concepts or theories we are holding on to "just because we were raised that way." I find that once I have an awareness behind the things

179

that are coming out of my mouth and/or "rules" I have glommed on to, it makes it easier to give myself some space to ask if I even mean what I am saying when I am in the thick of a parenting moment.

Continuing on with the **GRIT-workbook:**

1) Rules
   - What rules did you have when you were growing up?
   - Which of those rules have you chucked at the door?
   - Which of those rules are you holding on to? Why? Is it just because your parents had those rules, so you want to have them too? Do you even believe in them? How hard are they to enforce? - How much stress do they cause you when they don't work? Do you even need to hold on to them anymore?
   - What rules actually matter to you?

2) Expectations
   - What expectations did your parents have for you when you were growing up?
   - Where did those expectations help you?
   - Where did they hold you back?
   - Which ones were you resentful of?
   - How did your parents' expectations of you make you feel?
   - What expectations do you have for your kids?
   - Are they the same ones your parents had for you?
   - How are they different from the ones that were placed on you?
   - Why do you have these expectations?
   - Where do these expectations come from? (And do you even like/respect the person who planted that seed?)

3) Get in Their Shoes
   - When you were the same age that your kiddos are today, what do you remember about your worldview? Did you think you had it all figured out? Who did you think knew best? How can you take that knowledge and reframe how you talk with your kids?
   - Did you get really upset when your mom or dad assumed they knew you better than they actually did?
   - Did it frustrate you when adults did not take you seriously? Do you have any reason to believe that your kids would feel any differently?

What themes do you see emerging? What new mindset do you need to adopt when it comes to parenting? What insights do you have that you didn't see before? How do you plan on implementing what you are discovering so you are showing up as the parent you want to be?

Present

Being present at home is another pain point with my clients. Often work, work email, and work stress pour into time and mind when they are at home. And, let's face it, sometimes sitting down and playing with a three-year-old for hours on end sounds boring. The nails on the chalkboard kind of boring. So, you are sitting there, trying to play, trying to feel like a "good mom," but none of this feels "fun." This isn't what you thought motherhood would feel like. What does this mean? What is the vulnerable truth that so many professional moms face? That working is actually easier than parenting. Working can be more fun and rewarding than parenting at times. Yet, that doesn't give us permission to check out. More than ever, we need to be present. I know, don't kill me.

The good news is that we don't need to be present 24-7. Did you know that just fifteen minutes of super-focused, unstructured, child-led time with your kiddo might be all they need?[28] Also, recall what we already covered in chapter 5. Find your one way to plug into your family each day. Focus on that one thing and be 100% present and ready to win.

GRIT-work

GRIT-work in this section will feel familiar to what we did in chapter 5. Get out your **GRIT-workbook**, look back to see what you jotted down in earlier exercises and then ask these questions:

How will you plug into your family today? Can you set aside fifteen minutes for each of your kids? Can you put away your phone and work, look at them, ask them what they would like to do, and play the games, draw the pictures, and build the LEGOs *their way* for just fifteen minutes?

No More Martyrdom

When I run time-management workshops for law firms to help elevate their employees' time-management skills, I begin by establishing a physical and mental health baseline. As you know from chapter 5, these pieces are crucial to ensuring that new productivity skills stick. One of these presentations sticks out in particular. During the presentation, I had each attorney and staff member share their nutrition, movement, and mindset goals with the group. I felt a trickle of electric hope run through the room during the course of our workshop as each individual

---

28. Sarah Rosensweet, "Special Time," Sarah Rosensweet Peaceful Parenting, accessed July 13, 2023, https://www.sarahrosensweet.com/special-time/.

shared what she would focus on. As we were wrapping up, one of the women raised her hand and asked something along the lines of "But how do you get all of this done? How do you focus on your health, prepare healthy meals, workout, and also take care of everything else? My husband leaves for work at 3 a.m. and my daughter has soccer going late into the night, so when we get home, everything falls on me."

Upon further exploration with her, "everything" included washing, folding, and putting away laundry for her whole family, including her husband and her sixteen-year-old daughter. Upon even further exploration, we discovered that the reason she was still putting away her daughter's laundry was because said daughter did not feel like putting her clean laundry away. Instead, she would take all of the clean laundry and put it back in the dirty laundry, creating unnecessary work for Mom.

Then this mom said these intriguing words: "My daughter is making it so hard for me!"

While I felt for this mom and all of her frustration and agitation, change needed to start with her. As we dove more into this conversation and started troubleshooting, I pointed out kindly, "Mom, at the end of the day, *you* are giving yourself this extra work. It doesn't have to be this way."

"But she doesn't even know how to do the laundry."

"Trust me, if my eleven-year-old son knows how to do it, so can she. Besides, this is a life skill she needs to learn. I know how much you want to have more time for yourself, and I can tell you are so burned out and tired from working all day and running around to soccer all night. Your daughter wants a healthy mom who cares about herself.

The change begins with you. Can you talk with her tonight and explain the new way of doing things?" The audience nodded along with me.

Moms. We absolutely 100% cannot do it all. There is a great meme going around that captures the sentiment of this concept perfectly that I direct you to in the online resources. Take a moment and check it out!

I know you are tired. I know you have hidden in your closet just to cry. I know you have had toddler-style temper tantrums when it gets to be too much. Me too.

How do we chip away at what seems like a mountain? We lighten our burden. Unapologetically. We let go of wearing the need to be the martyr. We let go of feeling like the whole world will collapse if we don't do all the things. We rid ourselves of the fear of finding out who we truly are if we give away what we are carrying.

It will feel next to impossible to really dive into what we talked about in the earlier chapters if you don't start giving away some of the household things and chores that someone else in your family can (and should) be doing. Yes, even if they don't do it "right." Remember to ask yourself, each time you want to cringe and your hands are begging you to take over, "Are they doing it well enough?" That is all that matters.

For example, if the kids put their laundry away by shoving shorts and T-shirts into drawers when you would have lovingly folded each one . . . Does it matter? Does their underwear need to be folded? Truly? Does it really matter if the wrong bowls are stacked together, so long as you can find them? Does it matter if, when they go around the house collecting trash, they don't get every last piece from each recycling bin, so long as they take out the majority of it? Can the kids address their end-of-year cards to their teachers, even though their writing is barely legible? Can they wrap the present for the birthday party?

Can you make these small moves? I know this sounds dramatic, but your life depends on it.

I hereby give you permission to be selfish. Otherwise, you are selfless. Self-*less*. Less than self. How is that possibly okay?

If this is still a hard concept for you, think about the mark you want to leave for your daughter. Do you want to teach her that she must do all the things . . . perfectly? To put her physical and mental health on hold for everyone else? What about your son? Do you want to teach him that this is okay? Should he expect these things from his spouse? That he can go through life with everything done for him? Is that the man you want to raise? Our kids watch and listen to everything. If we can make our plate less full and be the example of a healthy parent to our kids, isn't it time to do so?

GRIT-work

Time to get out that **GRIT-workbook** and brainstorm some ideas to help lessen your load. It is amazing how giving some small things away lightens not only your physical load, but your mental load as well:

1) List all the chores you currently do around the house.

2) Pick three that you can give away (bonus points if they are ones you hate).

3) Plan a family meeting where you express your goal of getting healthy or having more time to yourself to maintain your sanity. If appropriate, talk with your partner first and have them be your ally in your meeting. In that meeting, share your chore list with your family and request that they take certain chores off of your plate. Try to maintain a balance of listening and also advocating for yourself. If an allowance is an appropriate conversation

here, weave that in.

4) Systematize the chores you are giving away by making sure the chore happens at the same time each day. Remember it by tacking it to the wall in plain sight.

I will leave you with one last example. Unloading and loading the dishwasher is the bane of our family's existence, mostly my husband's (I cook, he cleans). It gets so out of control that we flip that thing twice a day on a normal day. I had an epiphany one morning as I was running around the kitchen like a four-legged chicken with my head cut off, taking on the dishwasher because my husband was out early for work. I noticed that the kids were just sitting there, blissfully unaware and playing away on their iPads as they ate their breakfast. From that day on, at 7:45 every morning, Alexa rings her alarm and the kids know it is time to unload the dishwasher. That one act saves us so much time. We are about five months in, and the kids are on autopilot. So what if my measuring cups aren't perfectly stacked? They are clean and put away.

What chore can you give away? *Today?*

CHAPTER 11
Seeing in Color

"Unwritten," Natasha Bedingfield

Wiping Off the Lenses

One of my worst spirals began during a Friday night happy hour. We were celebrating finishing our first full month of law school at a popular Mexican restaurant across the street from the National Cathedral in Washington, DC. I was a half a pitcher deep in frozen strawberry swirled margaritas. My bestie from college was hanging out with me for happy hour, and we escaped to the bathroom so we could actually talk alone and catch up outside the ears of everyone else.

Before I knew it, our conversation went sideways, and I was freaking out and confessing to her that I did *not* belong in my class. Big margarita-fueled tears ran down my cheeks as I explained how *everyone* was smarter than me, I was too scared to raise my hand, I was surrounded by people who all seemed to know things I did not, and I was living a lie. I was so scared that someone would figure me out and then everyone would know I was a fraud. You can imagine my horror when, as I was mid-soliloquy, the door to one of the bathroom stalls squeaked opened and out popped one of the girls in my class. The nervous way she looked at me, and I at her, is seared into my brain. I had just dared to utter all of my truest feelings out loud, and I was overheard by one of the people who intimidated me the most. I wanted to crawl into a hole.

Eleven years had to go by before I had a name for the feeling: "Impostor syndrome."

My path to seeing in color began when I read Sheryl Sandberg's *Lean In.* She blew my mind when she recounted the speech given by Dr. Peggy McIntosh titled "Feeling Like a Fraud":

> *[McIntosh] explained that many people, but especially women, feel fraudulent when they are praised for their accomplishments. Instead of feeling worthy of recognition, they feel undeserving and guilty, as if a mistake has been made. Despite being high achievers, even experts in their fields, women can't seem to shake the sense that it is only a matter of time until they are found out for who they really are—impostors with limited skills or abilities.[29]*

Do you remember when you first heard about impostor syndrome and realized, "Oh my gosh, everyone else feels this way too?" Do you remember the incredible weight that lifted right off of your shoulders, and how it is like someone cleared the lenses of your glasses for the first time? Do you remember the first time you took a breath and realized that perhaps you *do* deserve that amazing position you have now? That you are 100% where you belong? That you are not a fraud?

---

29. Sheryl Sandberg, *Lean In: Women, Work, and the Will to Lead* (New York: Alfred A. Knopf, 2013), 28–29.

I am guessing that first ah-*ha* was sometime in your late twenties or thirties, or perhaps even in your forties. I am guessing that that was one of the first times you took a good look at the world around you and it looked . . . different. More vibrant. More beautiful. More clear. Connected. Perhaps the color tuned in a little deeper.

Giving a name to impostor syndrome and starting to leave it behind is Step 1. Just like you see in those late-night infomercials, though— but wait, there's more.

What Is a Self-Limiting Belief Anyway?

Just like impostor syndrome buries itself in our subconscious minds, so do what's called "self-limiting beliefs." Think of them like second cousins to one another.

Similar to how I can clearly recall when my impostor syndrome was at its peak, I can tell you exactly where I was when I learned the term "self-limiting belief" and how I felt when it started to evaporate in a great big poof of tears and "me too's."

The ah-ha occurred when I attended at a retreat in Destin, Florida, surrounded by many (many) beautiful women who all seemed to have it way more together than I did. There was a cool confidence floating around them, and it radiated out in everything they did—the way they dressed, talked, danced, and floated around the house. Most of all, I was weirdly jealous of their beautiful hair, which most of them worked up in these gorgeous, chunky braids, the ones you see on Pinterest and in wedding magazines. I don't know why that was the thing to send me down some weird rabbit hole, but it was. It didn't matter that I was probably one of the oldest people there or that I had a JD. Those credentials didn't really have a place in this group. Instead, I was left feeling rather "uncool" because I didn't feel as bright and shiny as everyone else appeared to be.

Not realizing it, I started spinning a story in my head that went something like,

> *I am so not cool. I might as well not talk. If I try to talk to her, she is going to look at me like the nerd I am. I will probably say something dumb, or I will stumble over my words. They are probably judging me because every word that comes out of my mouth is uncertain and sounds like jibber-jabber. I didn't wear the right clothes. They are probably wondering why I am even here and if I belong. What if I have no one to sit with? Oh gosh, this is all going to be so awkward. What if they are talking about me behind my back? I feel like I'm in elementary school all over again, when I never had the right bangs and I had to wear knock-off, dirty Keds. I am NOT going to open my mouth. I am just going to sit here and try not to gawk. If I stay small and quiet, no one will know I don't belong.*

Not only was I feeling a little sad because of my uncoolness, I was equally annoyed with myself that this shit still got to me. I was in the middle of really finding "me" again, and the fact that feeling "not cool enough" was *still* a thorn in my side made me wonder how far I'd actually come. Ugh.

And yet, just a few hours later, every single one of us women had tears streaming down our faces. Yes, even the women who were super cool and intimidating. Even the women with the most gorgeous chunky braids who seemed to float on air. It turns out there was a great equalizer: the concept of "enough."

That night, Calie, one of the retreat leaders led a group exercise to help us settle in and begin the retreat with a clean mindset. She began by asking us to write down three to five of our biggest fears. She then asked us, "If all of those fears were to come true, what would that mean about you?"

You could feel the mood shift immediately. It went from a giddy, silly, pumped-up vibe to a palpable heaviness within minutes. If you could have physically seen the energy in the room, you would have seen it shift from bouncing around on the tops of our heads to landing heavily in the pits of our stomachs. As we listed our fears and thought about what all of those fears would mean if they were true, our guards began to fall. We confronted the worst of it. And then we began to share.

It was like Calie had cast a spell. Every single one of our statements ended in an "enough." It was bizarre, until it wasn't.

In our sharing, I was quickly reminded that all of us women battle the same thing: our "enoughness." And that, my readers, is the essential part of a self-limiting belief—a statement we believe about ourselves, putting us down, that usually ends in "enough."

Let me share some of mine that I have struggled with throughout the years so you can see what I mean.

"I'm not cool enough."

"I'm not skinny enough."

"I'm not smart enough."

"I'm not articulate enough."

"I'm not original enough."

"I'm not a good enough mom."

How are these landing with you so far? If you have been worried that you are somehow deficient or weird because you talk to yourself this way or you have these beliefs, I can pretty much assure you that everyone else does too. Even those colleagues that seem super crazy confident, the ones that have all of their shit together. Even they have an "enough" statement lurking in them. In all of my time lawyering, mediating, and coaching, I don't think I have ever encountered anyone who did not have any of these "enough" thoughts.

What Do We Interpret These Statements to Mean?

These thoughts, these self-limiting beliefs, instill fear in us. Not a Freddy Krueger horror movie kind of scary, but scary nonetheless. As we begin to visualize and internalize these beliefs, we can physically feel the fear in the pits of our stomachs, the weight sitting on top of our chest, and the tension we hold in our shoulders. The self-limiting belief fear is the kind that chokes us and makes it hard for us to breathe. As our minds explore each self-limiting belief, our thoughts run so fast and far and wide that, before we know it, we are playing a movie in our heads of all of the awful things that will happen if the belief is indeed true.

It goes something like this:

I'm not cool enough. Therefore, no one will want to be friends with me, and I will never fit in. I will always feel lonely and bored and will always have to sit alone.

I'm not skinny enough. Therefore, I will never be attractive, and everyone will look at me and judge me in everything I wear. How am I ever going to find anyone?

I'm not smart enough. Everyone here is raising their hand all the time, and I am scared to raise my hand and talk because what if what I say isn't well-spoken enough/good enough/smart-sounding enough? What if I look dumb? What if I trip all over my words and people look at me, wondering how I got here anyway?

I am not articulate enough to be the lead trial attorney. The judge will wonder why my firm/organization put me in this position because I cannot recite the law fast enough, and I will get all flustered and stumbly. I will start shaking, my papers will fly everywhere, and I will annoy the whole courtroom.

I'm not original enough, and no one is going to care what I have to say or write because it has all been written and said before. Who cares if I said it a bit differently? Everyone is going to roll their eyes at me and this book and talk about me behind my back.

I'm not a good enough mom. If I were, my kids would listen more. Instead, when the kids act out in public, all the other parents are wondering what the heck I am doing and are thinking that I have zero control, so I must be a bad mom. Even worse, I am screwing things up as a mom, and my kids will end up hating me, and they won't want to hang out with me in their twenties—and what if our family never gets together as we all age?

Do you see how one little fleeting thought can explode into your very own major motion picture?

Did you also notice the theme in each self-limiting-belief movie? Let me give you a hint: "friends," "everyone," "everyone," "people," "judge," "courtroom," "everyone," "other parents." See the theme? Isn't it unreal that every single "enough" statement leads to a movie where we worry about how others view us? Who the heck is "everyone," anyway? Sometimes, the "everyone" that we are visualizing is people we don't even know and have never even met. Often, they are strangers. For all we know, we are worried about what a potential ax murderer thinks about us. Weird, right? Sort of silly, if you really think about it. Why are we constantly seeking the approval of everyone around us?

Not only do these self-limiting beliefs make us feel awful and make us want to just lie in bed under the covers and hide from the world, but they also hold us back. They block our potential. They keep us living in a world of fear (just like our brains do, as we talked about in chapter 6) so that we never actually put ourselves at risk and take that first step to what very well could be our technicolor life. Look what happens:

I'm not cool enough. Therefore, no one will want to be friends with me, and I will never fit in. I will always feel lonely and bored and will always have to sit alone . . . so I am not even going to try to have a conversation with that girl who seems too 'cool' for me. I would love to hang out with her because I think we would actually get along, but instead, I will just smile a tight smile and wave and not utter a single word because I am too scared she will reject me.

I'm not skinny enough. Therefore, I will never be attractive, and everyone will look at me and judge me in everything I wear . . . so I am not going to buy that super cute dress that I really loved and really felt good in. I hated how it showed parts of my body I don't love, so it is not worth the risk. While I am thinking about it, I am not seeing progress fast enough with my workout I have been doing these last few months, so there is no point in working out tomorrow. I would rather just put it off since I don't look the way that I want to look anyway. I am just going to sleep in and stop worrying about this. Who cares if it is 'healthy'? It is not like you can actually see any results anyway.

I'm not smart enough. Everyone here is raising their hand all the time, and I am scared to raise my hand and talk because what if what I say isn't well-spoken enough/good enough/smart-sounding enough? What if I look dumb? What if I trip all over my words and people look at me, wondering how I got here anyway . . . so even though I am pretty damn sure that I have a solution to the problem that no one else sees or has thought of yet, I am just going to keep my mouth shut. It is too scary to put myself out there.

I am not articulate enough to be the lead trial attorney. The judge will wonder why my firm/organization put me in this position because I cannot recite the law fast enough, and I will get all flustered and stumbly. I will start shaking, and my papers will fly everywhere, and I will annoy the whole courtroom . . . so I am not going to try. I am fine sitting second-chair to Tom. I don't mind doing all of the work, and even though I know this case inside and out and better than Tom does, it just isn't worth the risk. It is easier to hide behind him and let him take the credit. I mean, it would be really cool to make that opening statement, and I have always wanted to address the jury, but it is just too scary.

I'm not original enough, and no one is going to care what I have to say or write because it has all been written and said before. Who cares if I said it a bit differently? Everyone is going to roll their eyes at me and this book and talk about me behind my back . . . so why write it? What is the use? Why spend all of this time at the computer, with an aching back and dried out eyeballs, taking time away from my kids and friends? Is there any point? Why talk about it? If I talk about it, people might buy it, and then what if they judge me then? What if the people come after me in Amazon reviews? Oh God, then the whole world will know I am a failure! Maybe I should quit while I am ahead and not finish. The shame of a bad review will be too much to bear.

I'm not a good enough mom. If I were, my kids would listen more. Instead, when the kids act out in public, all the other parents are wondering what the heck I am doing and are thinking that I have zero control, so I must be a bad mom. Even worse, I am screwing things up as a mom, and my kids will end up hating me, and they won't want to hang out with me in their twenties, and what if our family never gets together as we all age? . . . So why try? If my kids already think the worst of me, I might as well keep being a yelling mommy. I got yelled at, and it got me pretty far in life, so I guess I can just keep yelling at the kids and they will go far too. And since I am so worried about all the other parents, I will just close myself off from them, not open up about how things are so hard, and avoid eye contact when I am at school functions. It is easier to just sit alone in my bubble.

Ouch, right? Do you see how each belief turns into a movie? Then the movie turns into worrying about being judged by others. Next, the fear of judgment determines the actions you take? Remember how we talked about being CEO of your workday in chapter 7? Why on earth are we letting others, sometimes mere strangers, be the CEOs of our entire lives?

Are you thinking about all of the times you have let a thought hold you back from something you really wanted? Are you ready to turn this around? Let's talk about how.

How to Address SLBs (Sorry Little Bitches)

First up, let's make it fun. No more are we calling these thought suckers "self-limiting beliefs." We are going to give them a new name—you ready? Let's call them "sorry little bitches."

That feels a lot better, doesn't it?

"Self-limiting beliefs" feels so sad and off-putting when you think about it. If we can call these suckers "sorry little bitches," or SLBs, I feel like we are already winning.

Next, I want to briefly explain *why* our brains do this nonsense thing. I find that when I know the why or what is behind something, it makes it easier for me to see it for what it is. Remember what we learned in chapter 6? Our brains are trying to keep us safe. Perhaps there was a time that something awful did happen. Perhaps you have now amplified that one event in your brain to be larger than it was, or to have more meaning than it did, and your brain and subconscious are saying, "Well, we don't want you to feel that again! That was awful! We need to keep you safe. No risk for you. Safe and boring is better. Stay here, stay comforted, stay stagnant. If you try to make a move, you might get hurt, and that is no good."

It's time to break the SLB cycle. It can be hard, and it will take work, but it will be worth it. It is likely not a one-and-done thing. It is a method that takes practice. You are human; SLBs will still hijack your day from time to time. SLBs still creep in on me too. The trick is to recognize it, work on it, and keep working on it, so the time we spend living in these movies, in a life of fear, and not taking the action we know we need to take becomes less and less.

But remember this:

If you can see it, you can name it. If you can name it, you can address it. If you can address it, you can flip it. If you can flip it, you do not need to be tied down by any of that anymore. You. Can. Be. Done. You can start to live your technicolor life.

Trick 1: Call BS

Recognize the SLB for what it is. Have some awareness that the thought that floated into your head is just one of those SLBs you read about. Ask yourself if you want your life to be limited in some way by *this* thought. Visualize yourself catching it (literally with your hand, like catching a lightning bug), look at it, and really examine it, like an outsider looking in. You might instantly call BS and say, "This is crap and not true." Taking a moment to have that awareness might be enough to allow you to acknowledge the SLB and let it go. If not, examine the belief you are holding in your hand as if you were the person who loves you the most on this planet.

Trick 2: Find the Evidence That the SLB Is a Big Fat Lie

If looking at the SLB in your hand and calling BS is not yet enough to vanquish it, it is time for you to go on a treasure hunt and find all the evidence from your past that proves the SLB is a big fat lie. Here, you do this exercise by stating your SLB and then writing down as much proof as you can to show it is not true. Write down as much as you possibly can.

"I'm not smart enough."

I would not be this far in life if I actually believed that. I flew through high school, struggled in college and turned it around to graduate with honors, and then excelled in law school. After that, I passed the bar exam, won cases, and got amazing reviews from clients and colleagues. There is no way I would be where I am right now if I was a dummy. I am

100% smart enough. Even if I don't have all of the answers right now, I am smart enough to know where to find them.

"I'm not a good enough mom."

I think about my kids from the moment I wake up until the moment I close my eyes. Every day, I think about how I can help them, what I can say to them to make them feel loved, how I can make them feel secure, and what services they might need to help them excel. I smile at them when they walk down the stairs in the morning, and I kiss their heads every night. I spend hours upon hours finding the right camps, the right teams, and the right activities for them. I spend hours reading to them, playing with them, helping them, cooking for them, and loving them. I may not always be perfect, and that is okay. They aren't asking me to be perfect; they are just asking me to be their mom, and I am the only person on this planet who has that title. The fact that I am even worrying about this, day in and day out, and taking action every day to be the very best mom I can be, is enough.

Trick 3: Flip the Movie

Isn't it interesting how every single belief leads to a movie inside of our heads? Before anything has actually happened, our brain shows us a preview of what is to come. When we play these movies, our subconscious actually believes the movie has already happened and is a true story. So, to take advantage of this, let's give our subconscious a prescription for what we want and how we want to feel.

Just like with Trick 1, I want you to catch the SLB with your hand the moment you feel it setting in. I want you to flip the statement. Then I want you to imagine a movie scene where everything goes right and the most amazing things happen, rather than your fears.

"I'm not cool enough."

I belong in this room. I give off equal airs of confidence and friendliness. I am who and where I am supposed to be. Just as I find value in these people around me, they find value in me as well. Instead of being intimidated by everyone here, I am ready to use my voice, and I am going to strike up a conversation with that absolutely beautiful woman across the room who seems to have it all together. I will start by getting to know her, and I will find out that we have a lot in common. In just a few minutes, we will be laughing like old friends, and all of these nervous feelings will evaporate. I will wonder what was holding me back in the first place. In years, this will all seem really silly. I will tell her how I felt when we first met, and we will laugh!

"I'm not skinny enough."

I am looking in the mirror and turning myself from side to side to admire my whole body. I love my curves. I love the silvery lines gracing my belly and hips that remind me that I am a powerful woman who grew a human. I love that padding I have around my hips that makes me extra luscious and protects me when I fall. I love how I feel when I'm under the sheets and I wake up and stretch out long. I am so thankful for my body that allows me to walk this earth and pick up my kids. I am so grateful that I can take a full breath. I love being able to run in the backyard and keep up with my family. I work out because it makes me strong, inside and out. This is what matters and why I keep going.

"I'm not original enough."

I am the only me on this planet. I am the only me who has had my background and experiences. This alone makes me original and one of a kind.

Trick 4: Make It Untrue

Sometimes, just every so often, a self-limiting belief smacks a little hard because it might be a little bit true. However, just because that SLB may have *some* grounding in reality, that doesn't mean it has to stay that way. You have the power to make the SLB untrue. You have the power to flip the script. In fact, you are the only one who can. No one else is going to wave a magic wand and do it for you.

"I am not smart enough at my job. I am missing knowledge in some key areas to really excel and complete my project."

While you might be telling yourself that you aren't "smart enough" on a certain subject matter relating to your job, it may just be that you lack the knowledge, and it is your responsibility to go acquire it. Don't wait for your boss or colleague to call you out. It is time to make this fact "untrue," and you need to roll up your sleeves and do the research. What exactly don't you know? Where do you feel like you have gaps? What do you need to know more of? Instead of worrying about whether you aren't intelligent enough (you are), worry about just taking the step to become more educated.

"I am not articulate enough. I stumble over my words, and then when I really get going, I ramble and talk way too fast. I am never going to get the hang of speaking in public. I will never be picked to give the presentation."

Maybe this is true right in this moment. Maybe you had a horrific experience when you were younger, and the thought of public speaking terrifies you and your nerves outrun your ability to form coherent sentences. Maybe you do talk way too fast. If being picked to give the presentation is your goal, and if having the skill of speaking in front of others matters to you, then you need to work on building that skill. Your homework is to find ways to get this experience. Perhaps you go over to social media and start practicing. See if it gets easier. Volunteer to be a reader at your church. Or, if you are ready to go all in, hire a speaking coach, go through the training, see where you can improve.

Seeing in Color

Remember how sparkle wakes us up & GRIT takes action? When sparkle wakes you up, it can be damn scary. sparkle might nuzzle you with her pesky but determined head and right away, you start worrying about the "enough" factor. Promise yourself you will give sparkle a chance to shine, that you will do everything in your power to tackle those SLBs so that you allow sparkle to grow and are able to get to the part where you take GRITTY action to see how it all plays out. That is step one to living a life "in color."

Step two? Taking the GRITTY action, even when you are scared and the SLBs want to hold you back.

sparkle & GRIT together? Recognizing your life for the sparkly, GRITTY, wondrous thing that it is. Remember how we talked about gratitude in chapter 5? Once you start looking in your yesterday to find gratitude, you start finding and seeing sparkle everywhere. You become more alive. When you are in the most delicious moments, you will say to yourself, "Oh my gosh, the goodness is happening right now! I am here. I am living this life! And, it is indeed technicolor. I am so glad I GRITTED my way here."

GRIT-work

Did any of your SLBs start to nag you as you read this chapter? Did one of my examples hit (too) close to home? It is time to open your **GRIT-workbook** and get to work with Tricks 1, 2, 3, and 4 to overcome this SLB once and for all. Ok, that is a lofty promise. Truth is, that SLB will continue to pop up every now and then, but the more often you put this work into place, the less and less these SLBs will be able to keep their hold on you. What does that mean? You do the work now. And. When that SLB inevitably rears his nasty little head, you return to your **GRIT-workbook** and do it again. In your **GRIT-workbook** answer the following prompts when it comes to a SLB:

1) Is this pure BS? Is this what my best friend would think of me?
2) What is the evidence that my SLB is a lie?
3) Flip the movie - what does the opposite of my SLB look like?
4) What is in my power to make this SLB untrue?

CHAPTER 12
Battle Cry

"Fight Song," Rachel Platten

It's All Connected

Why is all of this *so* important? Do you ever feel like you were put on this earth for "something more," but you don't know what that is? If you are not showing up as your best self, you aren't giving yourself a chance to make that a reality. And yes, *you*, my dear friend, matter. You matter so much.

Your "something bigger" doesn't have to lead to fame and notoriety. I have read so many books and listened to so many inspirational speakers that there have been times I have wondered, "What about the woman who doesn't want all of that? What if she doesn't want to be this huge big deal—what if she just wants to be the most amazing version of herself in her everyday life? Isn't that enough? Or what about the woman who is so tired, and her number one goal is not to pop off at someone that day? Isn't that enough?"

Yes! Of course it is. Everyone's version of why they are on this earth is different. I firmly believe that every action, word, and thought propels our universe forward. Do you remember the movie *The Butterfly Effect*? Do you remember how a small change could lead to an entirely different outcome and storyline? If you aren't familiar with the concept, the term "butterfly effect" was created by a MIT professor and scientist who hypothesized that a tiny variable, such as a flap of a butterfly's wings, could change an entire weather system and thus have the potential of causing, or even preventing, a tornado.[30]

Think of how all different ways the butterfly effect has already played out for you. Think of how one decision . . . one night out . . . one glance . . . one smile . . . one yes . . . one no . . . changed it all. Now consider that doing your part in your everyday life has its own butterfly effect. You owe it to humanity to show up as your best self—as much as you can—because you never know what your smile to the checkout lady at the grocery store may mean worldwide.

Why It Matters: Battle Cry

I hired my first life coach back in December of 2020. While working with Nakia, I did a good amount of homework, but the following passage is my most favorite thing I wrote. It is my mission statement and purpose. It is my *battle cry* that I am inviting you to. It is my why behind writing this book. This mission statement is my sparkle—it is my why.

---

30. Edward N. Lorenz, "Predictability: Does the Flap of a Butterfly's Wing in Brazil Set Off a Tornado in Texas?" (lecture, American Association for the Advancement of Science, Washington, DC, December 29, 1972), https://static.gymportalen.dk/sites/lru.dk/files/lru/132_kap6_lorenz_artikel_the_butterfly_effect.pdf.

Women need encouragement and a LIGHT. With better-rested and more empowered women, we have the duty to change and power the world (especially in the shit show we have going on now). We (as women) need to be ready for battle in our own way.

Do you remember the beginning of 2021? Just looking at January, that the coronavirus was still running rampant, the Capitol was stormed on January 6, and there was a shooting in Indianapolis? In 2021, everywhere we looked, we saw despair. This hit harder than the norm because we were a year into the pandemic and ready for the *light*, yet it just wasn't coming. Somehow, 2021 felt more bleak than 2020.

Writing this now, in 2023, we are just in a different shitstorm. The 2023 Nashville school shooting just happened. My family's dinner conversation last night consisted of my eleven-year-old telling us his plan that if a shooter came to his school, instead of "hiding" behind the glass transparent walls that make up his classroom, he would just jump out of the second-story window, even if a teacher got mad, because a broken leg is better than being dead. My nine-year-old daughter was trying to make sense of things—"How far away is Nashville?" "What if the shooter was working with a team?" "What if the team is coming here next?" "The kids that died were nine. I am nine." When my kids ask, "What if it happens to us and in our school?", I have lost my words to reassure them.

By the time you read this, other catastrophes will have come and gone. Unthinkable, frustrating, and maddening things. Sadly, I don't think we are done facing the question of what do we *do?* How do we as adults, parents, good citizens, make a difference and turn this nonsense around?

I wish I had the answers to all of this. I wish I knew how to end gun violence and school shootings. I wish I knew how to repair our country. I wish I had a cure for any kind of disease and sickness. But here is what I do know. I do know that if we don't get our acts together, there is no possible way we will start to see a difference in this world.

I am looking at you, dear reader, because *you* hold a piece to this puzzle. Maybe you are an amazing activist. Maybe you are an incredibly effective advocate, and you know what to say and to whom. Maybe you are an amazing graphic designer who can create beautiful images and memes to get your point across in seconds. Maybe you are a scientist. Maybe you are working in a lab. Maybe you are inspired in your own way to provoke thought and change, and you just haven't stepped up yet because no one has done it your way before and you are scared. Maybe you feel like you are "just" a mom, but you know you are raising the most incredible kids who will make the difference our world needs to see. Maybe you are simply carrying yourself around as your very best self and your smile or kind act toward someone else is the very thing they need to be inspired, motivated, or encouraged to take their next step to figure out the answers to these big questions. Remember the butterfly effect—we all matter. Every single piece of the puzzle is integral to creating the whole picture. It takes everyone.

Here is what I do know to be 100% true. I know that you cannot do any of those things, and we together cannot contribute to making this world a better place, until we both get our acts together. We make up the sum of all the things.

I ask you, *implore* you, to join our collective battle cry.

Let's say it again.

Women need encouragement and a LIGHT. With better-rested and more empowered women, we have the duty to change and power the world (especially in the shit show we have going on now). We (as women) need to be ready for battle in our own way.

It is about both the big-deal and the little-deal things. It is all connected. We are warriors. We are warriors at home. We are warriors at work. You know how they say to eat, train, and sleep like an athlete? Well, we are here to eat, train, and sleep like MF warriors. sparkle & GRIT warriors. And yes, you, *you* were made for this. You would not have picked up this book if you weren't.

Don't believe me? Try this on for size. Stand up and read it out loud.

I, as a woman, need encouragement and a light. I am an encourager of myself and others. I can be my own light and can shine it so brightly that it affects everyone and everything around me. When I allow myself to rest; when I allow myself to become empowered; when I allow myself to rise up as the most wonderful, beautiful, and capable version of ME, I am doing my part to make this world a better place for myself, my family, my friends, and those souls I have not yet met. This is my opportunity. This is my legacy. This is my responsibility. I am here for it. I am ready. It is time. I have the strength, stamina, and fortitude to grow and carry on the work my mother's mother's mother started.

GRIT-work

Break open your **GRIT-workbook**. Jot down what parts of my battle cry you want to take as your own. What else matters to you? What is the one thing you wish you could change in this world? How can you rewrite what I wrote and make it personal for you? What gets you going? Why does all of this matter? What makes you so passionate that it brings you to tears? What makes you so sparkly excited that you are ready to jump into GRITTY action?

Compass

Now that you have your battle cry (and if you are still working on it or not 100% sure about it, this next **GRIT-work** might give you further clarity—and I give you permission to work on the next exercise and then come back and see if you can refine your battle cry), we need to also construct your compass. Just as a compass always points north, your sparkle & GRIT compass will act as a gut check to ensure your thoughts, actions, and inactions are aligned with your battle cry. Your compass has four quadrants: work, family, health, and self. Once you are crystal clear on who you want to *be* and what you need to *do* (or again, *not* do) in these four areas of life, and at the same time have ensured that each serves your battle cry, your compass will serve as a reminder to point you in the right direction at every turn and help you approach any blessed thing that comes your way. This means that not only does this compass keep you aligned with your battle cry, but it also serves to ensure you are creating your version of work-life balance.

GRIT-work

Break open that **GRIT-workbook** and let's figure out how to infuse sparkle & GRIT into your life in a way that will last forever, help you define *your* version of work-life balance, and help you live out your battle cry.

We start with the four quadrants that show up again and again: work, family, health, and self. In each section, we need to ask three important questions:

Who do I want to BE? (sparkle)

What do I need to DO? (GRIT)

What are my values?[31]

1) Work

- Be
  - Who do I want to be at work? How do I want to carry myself?
  - What do I want to emanate?
  - What kind of boss do I want to be? (Perhaps think back in time to your favorite boss and draw inspiration from them.) How do I want my colleagues to view me? My team?
  - What kind of employee? How do I want my boss to view me? My team?

- Do
  - What kind of work do I want to do?
  - What sets my soul on fire?
  - What is a job well done?

- Values
  - What values mean the most to me at work? Public service? Leadership? Adventure? Excellence?

---

31. A full list of values is available in your **GRIT-workbook**!

2) Family
- Be
  - What sort of mom/parent do I want to be?
  - What sort of partner?
  - Who do I want to show up as for my family? (Perhaps think back in time to how you grew up, your friends' homes, your coaches. Draw from the very best of all of them.)

- Do
  - What sorts of things am I doing as a mom?
  - Am I the mom who hosts playdates, or the mom who drives kids around? Am I the mom on the PTA, or do I show up in a different way?
  - Where do I show up the most as a mom? What am I doing there?
  - Am I the wife who plans dates or the wife who nags?
  - Am I the wife who goes the extra mile to make sure we are connecting, or would I rather shut down?
  - Am I a wife who has been taken advantage of for too long? Where can I stand up for myself? What hard decisions do I need to make?

- Values
  - What values mean the most to me when it comes to my family? Affection? Loyalty? Freedom? Pleasure? Nature? Happiness?

3) Health
- Be
  - Do I want to consider myself a healthy person?

- What does being healthy mean to me?
- How else would I describe myself as a healthy person?

- Do
  - What do I *do* to be healthy?
  - Do I lift weights? Run? Practice yoga? Meditate? Breathe? Journal? Sleep?
  - Do I need to be following doctor's orders I have been ignoring? Do I need to be making the next appointment?

- Values
  - What values mean the most to me when it comes to my health? Excellence? Order? Physical challenge? Responsibility?

4) Self
- Be
  - Who do I want to *be*?
  - What is the essence of me?
  - If someone is describing me, how do I want to be described?

- Do
  - What do I want to *do* outside of work, family, and health?

- Values
  - What values mean the most to me when it comes to *me* that I have not yet named, but I know they have a place?
  - If I had to narrow down every single value to one, which one makes me feel the most *me*?

Now that you have laid the groundwork, it is time to create your compass in sentence form. We start with a few sentences that capture each quadrant. *Bold* or <u>underline</u> your core values. Use the following as an example.

Work: I want to feel good about the work I do and love my clients and their purpose. I want my work to have impact (**meaningful work**) and to approach each day with **optimism** and **curiosity**. I want to be a team **leader** who leads by examples, listens, and is **kind**. I want to be thought of as hardworking and organized.

Family: My family comes first. I want to be the mom who shows up to all of the school functions. I want to be the mom who shows **compassion** by listening to her kids with **curiosity** and **kindness**. My husband and I treat one another with **respect** and **loyalty.** We are the house where all the kids come for **fun** and **happiness.**

Health: I am a **healthy** person who works out with **determination**. I show up with **optimism**, and I make sure I am having **fun**.

Me: I am **compassionate** and **curious**. I approach my friends with a lack of judgment and show them **kindness** and **loyalty** at every turn. I make time every day for **fun**.

Let's boil all that down into a few sentences:

> *I am a **healthy, fun**-loving, **curious** mom, wife, coach, and mediator. I approach each day wondering what life will put in my path, and I am **determined** to approach each new opportunity with **optimism** and **kindness**, no matter what life brings.*

Now, add your battle cry to the end to really make it *pop!* and feel bigger than just you. Feel free to riff off of mine. Seeing it all together:

*I am a **healthy**, **fun**-loving, **curious** mom, wife, coach, and mediator. I approach each day wondering what life will put in my path, and I am **determined** to approach each new opportunity with **optimism** and **kindness**, no matter what life brings.*

Women need encouragement and a LIGHT. With better-rested and more empowered women, we have the duty to change and power the world (especially in the shit show we have going on now). We (as women) need to be ready for battle in our own way.

Make sure you write out your compass and battle cry and store them somewhere easy for you to see and remember (a sticky note is a great option!). The next time you don't feel totally aligned with a request that has been made of you or an action you are about to take or just feel a general unease, read your compass and battle cry and remember who you are and what you stand for. If you are invited to a committee or to serve on a board where these values aren't recognized or appreciated, say no. Say yes to the opportunities that come your way that allow you to do any of these things.

If you need to jump in the pool with your kid, despite the fact you blow-dried your hair that day, do it anyway (**fun**).

If you find yourself gossiping about the neighbor down the street, stop it (**kind**).

If you approach a colleague or new client (or even opposing counsel), make an effort to start asking questions and really understand where they are coming from (**curious**).

If you find yourself reaching for a glass of wine instead of waking up early to finish your blog post that you know will inspire others, go to bed (**determined**).

215

What other ways can you see your compass working for you? What things do you know you need to say yes to right now? What is a hard no that you need to remember?

When your compass and battle cry are complete, I would *love* it if you shared it with the world. Make it pretty. Make it pop. Share it on social media. Tag #sparkleandGRIT. Let the world see the beautiful, wondrous creature you are!

CHAPTER 13
Work-Life "Balance"

"Come Tomorrow," Dave Matthews Band

If you skipped all the other chapters to come and read this one because this chapter is why you bought the book, surprise! You know how some hotels don't have a thirteenth floor? This book is missing a "full" chapter 13.

Why? Because every single concept and lesson you have learned thus far and all of the **GRIT-work** you have completed are in fact the keys to determine what work-life "balance" looks like for you. In order to truly beat burnout, find balance, and *finally* live that technicolor life you are aching for and deserve, it is necessary to read *all* the other chapters in this book. There isn't going to be a chapter with the secret to work-life balance because that is what this whole book is about. Also, some people—a lot of people—will tell you that there is no such thing as work-life balance, and while I get what they are saying, I don't entirely believe that either. There is 100% work-life balance; it just looks different day to day, week, month, year, hour, minute, and second. You do not reach a pinnacle and say, "I am here! I did it! And now I am done!" Life is, and will just always be, a constant balancing act. Some days it will be really hard, because hey, life is in fact hard.

And, with the tools you learn in this book, you will recognize a hard day for what it is and be able to move on from it and get back to your sparkle & GRIT life.

The demands of work and family and life and self-care are ever-changing. So perhaps, instead of trying to find "balance" to get to an end result, can you try on the notion that your life is a masterpiece and your goal is harmony? That when you are living in harmony, you will feel a sense of balance because you are where you need to be at that moment in time?

Have you ever thought about the goal of "work-life" balance? What does it even look like if you have it? If I had to pick one thing, it would be to be able to breathe. A full breath, with no pangs or longing that I am not somewhere else that I should be. My goal behind this book is to give you the tools you need so you also can get to that feeling. When you are at work, you are *killing it* at work. When you are home with your kids, you are *actually present* with them. When you take time to yourself, you *enjoy* it. You do each of these things without hesitation and without guilt for not doing the other things you know you have on your plate. And how do you do that? By doing the groundwork we laid down already:

1) Remembering the best version of you (chapter 4);
2) Developing a morning routine, adding just one thing in at a time (chapter 5);
3) Practicing future-casting everyday (chapter 6);
4) Approaching work as the CEO (chapter 7);
5) Spending time finding and assessing friendships (chapter 8);
6) Taking care of your health (chapter 9);
7) Ending the martyrdom (chapter 10);
8) Seeing in color and overcoming SLBs (chapter 11);

9) Creating a battle cry and compass, a way for you to determine how to act and how to approach any given situation (chapter 12);
10) And remembering your pals sparkle & GRIT—for any situation, ask yourself, "How can sparkle & GRIT guide me through this?"

The sum of all these things is what helps you define and manage the concept of work-life balance. By remembering the best version of you and then taking steps to be that person again, you become more comfortable in your skin and in your daily actions. When you feel like the most true "you," everything else feels a little easier and you find yourself on firm footing and are "balanced" in who you are. When you have a tried-and-true morning routine, you are setting up each day "balanced" and ready. You set up each day with a road map of exactly who you need to be and what you need to do. Rather than your mind teeter-tottering all over the place, you are set and ready to go—"balanced." When you practice future-casting, similar to finding the most true *you*, you are also aligned with the *who* you want to be that day, again allowing you to breathe in the moment, knowing you are ready for what life will throw at you, and you are less likely to lose your "balance" when life throws you curveballs. When you approach work as the CEO, *you* are in charge, "balancing" the workload in a manner that is most beneficial to you. When you take the time to assess your friendships, you ensure that you have the right people surrounding you, thereby creating a network and community that holds you up when you feel off-"balance." These same people breathe life into you, helping you restore your sense of "balance" when you most need it. When you take care of your health, you restore "balance" to your physical and mental health. When you become the parent you want to be and stop feeling bitter about your parenting situation, you achieve a sense of internal peace, you enlist your family for help around the home, and you have a sense of "balance" at home. When you begin to see in color and let go of all of those SLBs holding you back, you approach life-changing opportunities with radiant confidence and make the most of them, restoring "balance" to your innermost self. When you have a battle cry and compass directing the way at every turn, you are reminded time and time again what "balance" looks like to you and you have an easier way to maintain it.

Do you see how all of these things work together to restore balance in every way, thus ultimately helping you create work-life balance? Do you see how each piece to the puzzle builds balance and, when they are added together, work-life balance is created? Do you see how it may change and shift but that, if you keep coming back to these concepts, your overall self will feel balanced at home, at work, and in life? Over time, and as you develop each of these skills, muscles, and mindsets, yours will become a life of harmony and you will no longer waste mental energy worrying about how to "balance" it all anymore. Instead, you will just be doing it naturally.

sparkle & GRIT MASCOT

Are you ready for a cute and fun visual that will remind you of everything sparkle & GRIT? Finally, the time has come where I get to introduce you to the sparkle & GRIT mascot: the flamingo!

Why the flamingo? Because she, too, is always in a state of balance. She alternates legs to ensure that she distributes and conserves her body's resources, just like how we must approach life. What is really interesting about the flamingo? When she locks one leg into place, she becomes even more steady and sways less.[32] Perhaps she is not "balancing" as much as determining what is most important in that moment to restore harmony within herself. Once she has mastered that, it all becomes easier. Thus, not only is the flamingo the perfect example of self-preservation, but she is also the perfect reminder that when we are singularly focused on one task, it is not only easier, but we do a "better" job at it.

If you had to take one thing away from this mini chapter, other than a reminder of the tools you already have to work on your version of work-life balance and harmony, I want you to visualize the flamingo. Stand tall. Stand graceful. Know you are 100% where you need to be at that moment. Know you are using your efforts in the exact right way at the exact right time. And smile, because hey, how can you not when you are thinking about a flamingo?!

---

32. Reuben Westmaas, "The Real Reason Flamingos Stand on One Leg," Discovery, August 1, 2019, https://www.discovery.com/nature/Reason-Flamingos-Stand-One-Leg.

CHAPTER 14

Wrapping It Up in a Nice Big Bow

"The Middle," Jimmy Eat World

Obstacles

We have done a lot of really important and amazing work together. *Yes!* I am so proud of you! I am imagining us jumping up and down, dancing, high-fiving, and you feeling *great* about this new sparkle & GRIT way of life! You cannot wait to start! You are ready for your world to become technicolor *now!*

And . . . I can pretty much guarantee that, just when everything is going right, something will happen to knock it all down, and you will slip up and fall into old patterns.

It happens. While we both know that you have superwoman blood running through your veins, you are also a human being. Humans are fallible. But our fallibility is also arguably one of our greatest gifts.

. . . Wait, what? I thought you were talking about obstacles, and now you are talking about gifts? I am confused.

Yes. Screwing up is 100% a gift.

When we fall off the horse, we are blessed with the reminder of how it *feels* to live life the old way. We remember what it is like to wake up foggy, to approach the day without an affirmation or a plan, to lose our overall sense of purpose, and to feel adrift. As a few days or weeks go by, we start to feel lost, edgy, sad. We have the *gift* of seeing and feeling just how different (and how much better) things are when we do the hard work and do the things we know bring sparkle & GRIT into our lives.

Where we were perhaps annoyed about the GRITTY step after GRITTY step we needed to take to get closer to a sparkly self, we find that perhaps the true sparkle is *in* the GRIT. We find that when we put in the work, try as we might fight it, we breathe a whole lot easier.

Screwing up is not failure. It is a gift to remember how things were before you had sparkle & GRIT in your life.

And . . .

Falling off the horse does not give you permission to stay sitting in that mud pile on the ground. It is your right, purpose, and obligation to stand up, dust off, and get back down to business.

GRIT-work

When you fall off the horse, crack open your **GRIT-workbook**, flip through the pages, look at all of the **GRIT-work**, read through your answers, and find your sparkles. Remind yourself of who you are and who you want to be.

I have included a "Break in case of emergency" worksheet in your **GRIT-workbook**. When the time is right, flip open to that page and GRIT it out.

How Are You Going to Celebrate and Feel Your Wins?

My dear reader, you are at the end of this book!
By now you have . . .

1) Defined your version of Groundhog Day;
2) Defined a version of your ideal world;
3) Developed a morning routine;
4) Began future-casting at home and at work;
5) Developed a habit of starting the workday with three "to-do" tasks each day;
6) Become the CEO of your day;
7) Conducted a friendship assessment;
8) Scheduled your health appointments;
9) Found new ways to be healthy on a day-to-day basis, likely cutting down on alcohol or sugar;
10) Given yourself grace as a mother;
11) Gotten rid of some household chores that are holding you back;
12) Identified and conquered any self-limiting beliefs that are holding you back;
13) Adopted a battle cry;
14) Created a compass.

By going through these exercises, you have developed your version of work-life balance.

For every *win* that you can see in the list above, I want you to get up right now and do a little dance. I want you to celebrate. I want you to dance around the house like a wild woman, pop some bubbly or sparkling water, and shout your victories. I want you to turn up the music and dance. Invite your kids, your partner, your mom. Let them dance with you. Let them celebrate with you. *You* are meant to be celebrated! Tell them your wins and why they matter. Take the time to treat this like a big deal—because it *is* one.

As for the GRIT-work you saved for later or don't have down quite yet? Bookmark and sticky note this book! Write on it. Underline it. Give yourself directions for what you need to do and when to do it. Put a note in your calendar and pledge that you will get GRITTY when you promised yourself you would. We have some work to do and some wins to celebrate. These things take time. It is imperative that you commit to when you are coming back.

My wish for you

Dear friend and reader, my wish for you is that you have embraced all things sparkle & GRIT and have embraced and fallen in love with this concept in a way that works deep within you. That you have put the time and energy into the **GRIT-work** and you are beginning to see the various shades of gray in your life transform into technicolor. To know that even if you fall down or feel hopeless on some days, sparkle & GRIT is within your reach—sparkle is there ready to nudge you with her sparkly head and GRIT will help stand you back up and get you moving in the right direction. That you feel securely armed with your compass and that you are ready to carry out and live your battle cry. That you are breaking free from monotony. That you are beating burnout. That you feel like you are finally finding out what work-life balance means to you.

FINAL GRIT-work

I never dreamed that sparkle & GRIT would evolve into what it is today. Part mindset, part nervous system regulation, part habit, part visualization, part rose-colored lens. My hope is that the next time you are approached with a difficult situation, whether big or small, you think to yourself, *How can I apply some sparkle & GRIT here? How can I use sparkle & GRIT to keep me going, to reframe, to spur me into action, to get me excited, to deal with this tough thing ahead of me?* The beauty of sparkle & GRIT is that *you* get to decide how you want to use it and how to best invite it in and make it turn your life into the technicolor dream you deserve it to be.

My ask of you: When you do use sparkle & GRIT, I want to know about it! I would love to see it in action. If you have already seen it work wonders in your life, stop what you are doing and let me know right the heck now! I am dying with anticipation to hear how you are living your technicolor life. Send me a message. Drop me a line!

If you are on social media, please do me the honor of tagging me in your post about your sparkle & GRIT win, and give it the hashtag #sparkleandGRIT.

IG: wendy_s_meadows
                sparkle_and_grit
LinkedIn: https://www.linkedin.com/in/wendy-s-meadows/

Thank you, truly, from the bottom of my heart. xoxo.

Next Steps

Join me!

If you are ready to join my free sparkle & GRIT Facebook community to connect with other like-minded individuals, please join us over there (there is a link to join in the resources). My hope is that we share our sparkly and GRITTY wins. We lift each other up. We battle together. We join hands, doing our parts to make the world better and to breathe easier, and we are the harmonious and collective *light* this world needs.

Connect with me!

Email: wendy@wendysmeadows.com (be sure to put sparkle & GRIT in the subject line!)

IG: wendy_s_meadows
sparkle_and_grit

LinkedIn: https://www.linkedin.com/in/wendy-s-meadows/

Grow with me!

Ready for 1:1 coaching? Head on over to www.wendysmeadows. com and book a call with me.

Group coaching more your thing? I got you. Book a call and let's chat!

Want me to come speak to your local organization? I would be delighted! E-mail me at wendy@wendysmeadows.com (be sure to put SPEAKING in the subject line!)

Remember . . .

If you read this book from cover to cover and skipped over the **GRIT-work**, it is time to get down and dirty. Remember to visit https:// wendysmeadows.com/sparklegritbook to download your workbook. If you would rather save yourself the headache of printing it out and want a spiral-bound copy instead, check out the resources section to purchase.

Acknowledgments

This part of the book feels like an award acceptance speech! How can I not start by thanking the original sparkle & GRIT team? There are too many of you to name, and I am nervous I will forget one of you! To all the sweaty selfies, Saturday morning calls, going Premiere two years in a row, pre-workout dance parties, and most of all, the connection, love, and sparkle you all showed one another and me. You are each truly all things sparkle & GRIT, and the idea of this book would not have been possible without you.

I am so incredibly grateful for my friend groups who have lifted me up over the years. There is something special that happens when these groups form and grow. These women are my lifeline and sounding board. To the AHS chic click (we never could spell that right!), the Bare Your Souls Club (both iterations), the Baha Tangas, and finally, the Fab 5. Lauren, Rachel, Rachael, Rebecca, and Eliz. Amy, Danielle, and Beth. Alex, Renee, Marla, and Tamara. Katie, Donna, Karis, and Jackie. The energy and love each of you have shown me throughout all the years, no matter what, means the world to me. You are more than friends; you are family.

Thank you to the one and only Jake Kelfer. You are a *force!* The minute I saw you run onto the stage, I knew I had to work with you. You have something special, and I am amazed by your abilities, your tenacity, and how you go deep fast and tell it like it is. You offer so much clarity in a world of confusion. I feel so lucky I listened to that podcast that brought me to Arizona and to meet you!

A HUGE thank you to my editors, Cory Hott and Yna Davis. Cory, you "got" me right away and got my brain straight early on in the process. I know I fought you at first, but how you helped me rearrange my ideas was spot on. Thank you. I miss our chats, and you better believe we will have that treasure hunt one day! Yna, your editing brought me so much joy, clarity, and inspiration. Your thoughtful notes, cheerleading, gracefully pointing out my faux pas, and excitement for my manuscript were the sprinkles on top of this whole process. When I began this endeavor, I was worried that I was missing a "safety net" in terms of catching myself and mistakes I could not see because I was too far into the writing process. You were 100% the person I needed at the end of this journey. Thank you. Together, you two are the dynamic duo!

To my four parents. To my mom, for being a forever constant and for loving me always. To my dad, for being a teacher since day one and for guiding me with love. To Jeremie, for giving me the gifts of space, time, and patience. To Al, up there biking around in Heaven—things weren't always easy (in fact, I would say they were pretty damn hard), yet you also made me "me," an enigma I am still trying to figure out. To all of you: now that I have kids the age I was when our family was in transition, I understand a lot more. Thank you for giving me the space to tell my story as I see and remember it. For pushing me when it was time. For believing in me always.

Last but not least—to the family I yearned for since I was a little kid. Thank you to my husband, Kirk. I already told the whole world how I feel about you in my dedication, but if you ever forget, go over there and read it again. And most of all, to my kids. You remind me every day how to sparkle & GRIT. You show me fun new ways to sparkle, and you *are* my sparkle when mine feels burned out. You reignite me, and your belief in me as your mommy is the light to my life. Thank you for giving me the office time to be able to GRIT this book into existence. Thank you for your surprise sticky notes and kind words. Thank you for giving me the same advice and encouragement I give you when I most need it. You two are every bit sparkle & GRIT and I could not be more proud of each of you.

Thank you For Reading My Book
And Learning All About
sparkle & GRIT!

Thank you for reading my book and all your effort with the **GRIT-work**. It 100% will make a difference in this world, and I am so excited to experience the butterfly effect of it. If you have any feedback on where I can make this book even better, please share it with me. If there is a line or passage that really resonated with you, please let me know that as well!

I have one last request for you! I would be thrilled if you left me an honest review on Amazon. This is my first book, and public ratings and reviews help me establish myself as an author. Meaning I need your GRITTY help to make me a sparkly success in the field of writing and publishing.

Thank you and to all those who sparkle & GRIT,
Wendy

About the Author

Wendy S. Meadows is a family law attorney turned life coach, who specializes in getting her clients unstuck so that they can achieve their professional and personal goals. Named as one of the *Top 100 Lawyers in Maryland*, and with over 20 years of combined experience in litigating, meditating, coaching and consulting, Wendy offers highly relatable and spot-on insight. Today, you will see Wendy coaching clients, consulting for small firms, speaking at events, and mediating family law disputes. In her free time, she enjoys playing in the water with her family and dreaming up her next travel extravaganza. Connect with Wendy at wendysmeadows.com.

Made in the USA
Middletown, DE
03 February 2024

48433202R00136